T0281918

Published by Semiotext(e)
PO BOX 629, South Pasadena, CA 91031
www.semiotexte.com

Cover Design: Faye Orlove
Layout: Aldon Chen

ISBN: 978-1-63590-227-3

Distributed by the MIT Press, Cambridge, Mass., and London, England
Printed and bound in the United States of America.

10 9 8 7 6 5 4 3 2 1

HOW TO FUCK LIKE A GIRL

Essays

Vera Blossom

CONTENTS

Being trans is a prayer for and belief in something better.
—Carta Monir

REMEMBER YOU'RE A GOD

You'll feel like no one wants you. The truth is you're a god, a miracle. People daydream of a big woman, a strong woman. They daydream of someone with a deep voice and a loud laugh. People wish they could be with women even though they crave cock. People wish they could be anything, and you have shown them that they could if they were brave. It's natural to love you. The truth is you'll go out into the world and wonder where you'll fit in. You miss the attention and the pleasure of gay men, of cruising in gay male spaces, and maybe you can't do that anymore. You'll feel at home in a sea of dykes, but you probably won't get laid there either. It's okay. Your power comes from your believers. Remember people love you, even if they only think of you in the dark of their room, kneeling at their bed. You're a god.

They'll say, "Drag is not dangerous" and, "Trans people don't want to hurt you." The truth is, we are. We do. The truth is, we want to destroy this whole joint and start over. Truth is, this party's dead, girl, and we want to find the next spot. We're doing a ritual outside and we're summoning lightning and thunder and brimstone so that the marble columns holding this sad little empire up will crack, and all of us will come tumbling down. I may be a god, but I've got the devil on speed dial. The truth is, I'm a monster and a freak. Truth is, you are too.

TRY OUT FAGGOTRY

Here's the truth: at some point I missed being a boy. Being a boy was so much easier than being a girl in so many ways that I could have never anticipated. For as long as I can remember, I wanted to be a girl. Even before I knew what it meant to be a girl—what a girl even was—I wanted it.

I wanted to be pretty and to be adored in the way that only femmes could be adored. Seeing a beautiful femme out in the world was—is—like getting a glimpse of a god or a fairy in the woods. Femmes have this air of knowing something, something more, more than you, more than me. Seeing a femme reminds you why people weave together stories of powerful, complex goddesses who enact their will upon the laws of physics. Look upon a high femme and it becomes easy to understand why humans have eternally built statues of giant women and erected temples around them to pray in. I've always desperately wanted to channel that goddess energy—to even just hold a fraction of it would be enough. To this day, years into my transition, I still revel in girlhood.

But I do miss being a boy. I miss being a gay boy to be completely clear. A faggot. Manhood—I shiver at the thought of it—was completely alienating. At least, the kind that I saw growing up. I never knew how to be that kind of man. I did know how to be a faggot.

I knew how to walk through a gay sauna and offer myself up to other, hungry men. I knew how to have sex crouched down in an alley or kneeled over in an empty house. I knew how to squat on a toilet in the men's bathroom at Whole Foods so it looked like only one person was in a stall and suck cock without getting caught. I knew how to comfort my girl friends the way I wished other men would for me, listening, hugging, laughing. I knew how to see a beautiful dress. I knew how to buy a nice button-up shirt. You know, fag shit.

When I crossed that invisible threshold—people could tell. I think this is true for every trans girl out there: even before you pump yourself full of estrogen or silicone or get a doctor to cut away the parts you don't like, you start to carry yourself differently. A switch flips inside your soul, and you start emanating a secret girl-mode signal so strong that you could walk to someone's house with a full beard and a hairy chest, in little running shorts and a tank top, but still, when 7.5LatinUncut fucks you, he's overcome with the urge to call you *baby girl*. Before you even know what 2.0 mg of estradiol looks like, men will say, "I don't know—something about you reminds me of those androgynous models you see in magazines," and you'll hold that comment close to your heart and try to remember it when you feel ugly.

This is how I began my foray into girlhood: with lots of sex.

Some of my earliest spellcrafting happened while I was fucking strangers. I'd imagine myself playing the role of an ingénue, the dumb slut in a porn video, the horny girl in a movie. Then, I'd go and fuck a big strong man, the kind of dude who leaned into toxic machismo, who liked to feel like a big strong man.

Don't get me wrong, I was always a romantic, hoping for some meet-cute where I'd find someone in real life and we'd play out a sweetheart romance like in the movies. Instead, I found intense psychosexual relationships with lesbian-adjacent classmates and an internet boyfriend who was too old for me. These were the people I could meet in my day-to-day life in Las Vegas. Hence, Craigslist.

Alone in my bedroom, I made a new reality come into being. The kind of reality where I was not a sad, lonely art school burnout and college dropout. Instead, I was a beloved slut with men clawing to be with me. With the correctly worded advertisement, I'd have dozens of emails in my inbox from men in the city who wanted a piece of me. I felt desired.

At this point, most of my friends had left the city for college on scholarships or moved away from their parents to try and make a life for themselves in Vegas. I was simply someone who dropped out of college on Orientation Day—I took my photo, got my printed university ID, got into my car, and withdrew from all my classes.

That is all to say: I was feeling self-destructive and in need of anything to make me feel better. I was too much of a square to binge drink and did not know where I would be able to get drugs, so I turned primarily to sex.

I found a lot of my first sexual experiences in the pages of Craigslist Personals (rest in peace)—Craigslist ads are a kind of manifestation ritual. Write the magic words into a secret book and voilà: cock!

My secret to getting laid was playing up my assets: young, dumb, and Filipino. I played up my twunky[1] youth. *Inexperienced bottom seeks pleasure. 20. 6 feet tall. 215 pounds. Filipino.* I made it easy to imagine a tan, fit hunk looking to get smashed rather than what I felt like, an awkward body, meat clumped on the bone, lanky. I lied about my age, too, adding another year to my real age. The inexperienced part felt true at least.

---

1   Twunk is a portmanteau of twink and hunk. As in, a little too chunky and big to really look like a twink, but not really beefy enough to be a bear or svelte enough to be an otter. If you don't know what a twink is, I think this book might be beyond your reading level.

Reading my old Craigslist ads now feels painful. I didn't even know who I was, yet I could discern that I possessed certain superficial qualities that other people saw as valuable, so I added them up and put them on sale. I was so hungry, so desperate for physical touch, the heat of another body pressed up against mine, that I'd remix my profile, add new details. Make myself younger or older, fib on my ethnicity—jump over a few kilometers so I wasn't Filipino but Thai or Japanese, with German or English heritage mixed in. I could be six feet tall or believably six foot three. If I was feeling petite, maybe five foot ten. I'd be 200 pounds or 250. Whatever attracted more attention, I'd just fudge; these were details that someone couldn't really figure out anyway. They were projections of what I imagined they wanted. It feels so reductive to dissect oneself into categories like this, but the gay hookup scene—as it perhaps always has been—was focused on bodies seeking bodies for sexual catharsis, not really on people seeking people. If you wanted to get off, you better accurately (or at least idealistically) describe your own puzzle piece so you could find the one you wanted to fit together with.

One desert autumn, or at least what we pretend is autumn in the desert, I put my feelers out in the Personals looking for a distraction from my under-stimulating community college drawing class that I thought I was too good for.

xxxxxxxxxxxxxxxxxxxxxxxxxxxxxxxxxxxxxxxxxxxxxxxxxxxxxxxxxxxxxxxxxxxx

Title: Young Asian wants to feel like a girl
Body: 20-year-old college student seeks masculine top to have some fun with. I'm Asian, six feet tall. I like to feel feminine.

xxxxxxxxxxxxxxxxxxxxxxxxxxxxxxxxxxxxxxxxxxxxxxxxxxxxxxxxxxxxxxxxxxxx

Describing my body so explicitly, so concretely, was painful and necessary. I'd tried being ambiguous before, leading with vibes and personality, only to be strung along by some guy who realized he did not, in fact, want to fuck an effervescent, large and in charge Jungle Asian. There were a few people in my inbox, mostly very old men with fetishes for Asian boys who were too young for them. I was not above sleeping with a chaser or fetishizer, and desperate for cock, so I was happy to use whatever asset I had to get my foot in the bedroom door.[2] Plus, it's not like I used to treat the men I slept with any better. The way I browsed through my Craigslist replies is the same way I look at take-out menus. I'd be in the mood for someone old or someone even older, someone fat or someone muscular, someone nerdy or someone athletic. If I wanted my dessert (like, let's say, a macho beefcake of color with a meaty cock), I'd have to offer the appetizer (tall Asian boy of indeterminate gender, eager to give head).

Among the ugly creeps I had no interest in fucking and the ugly creeps I did have an interest in fucking, there was someone who genuinely caught my interest. Not ugly. Creepy, maybe. He was married and "discreet" which basically meant he was doing some shit on the down-low.

xxxxxxxxxxxxxxxxxxxxxxxxxxxxxxxxxxxxxxxxxxxxxxxxxxxxxxxxxxxxxxx

From: Plinio Sanchez
        >> Hey bud,hot Latino gonna shower and grab a drink..u wanna join me??send a face pic in return and I'll send one..married discreet here.

xxxxxxxxxxxxxxxxxxxxxxxxxxxxxxxxxxxxxxxxxxxxxxxxxxxxxxxxxxxxxxx

---

2   As of writing, I am still considering whether or not I am above this.

We exchanged face pics and he proved he was not lying. He was indeed hot and Latino. Sure, his picture was blurry, maybe a little outdated, but at least at some point between the invention of digital cameras and the email he sent me in 2015, his biceps were bigger than my head, and he was good looking. I could suck someone's dick who used to be good looking. If he happened to be *presently* good looking and maintaining a bicep curl routine, well that was just gravy.

Plinio sent me his phone number so that we could migrate our conversation from Gmail to iMessage. In hindsight, this was decidedly less discreet, especially for someone who was hiding his adulterous blowjobs from his wife. But I was nineteen, horny, and not interested in drawing still lives anymore, so I drove my gay ass to some nouveau riche housing development in East Las Vegas. With a shred of anxiety and fear of a righteously angry wife in my heart, I parked at the edge of the neighborhood, forcing me to walk about ten minutes from my car to his house. Having some faggy artist type marching around his neighborhood was probably not his idea of discreet, although it seemed like discretion was out the window at this point. He met me at his front door half hard, greeting me with a question:

"Do you want this fucking dick?"

According to my own increasingly hard dick, I did.

I followed Plinio into his McMansion, feeling the floor change from quartz tile to plush carpet under my busted Doc Martens. Plinio's grand house tour ended abruptly. He sat down a couple feet from the front door, in the front room that evidently served as a combination home office and playroom. On one wall sat an austere IKEA desk, beneath which a hefty Dell computer towered from the ground. On top of it: a skinny monitor displaying several tabs of Plinio's recent porn searches. My beefy DILF quickly kicked away a couple of loose toys on the ground, vaguely in the direction of a large toy chest sitting against another wall.

I knelt in front of him, fully clothed, and got to work. While I like giving head, I wanted to get off too. I reached down to rub one out myself, managing to pull my pants down while kneeling in hefty fucking leather boots.

We met like this several times and, luckily, I never met his girlfriend/wife or his kids. Looking back, the entire relationship was pretty much a one-way street. Pliny never returned the favor to give me head, we never kissed, he never fucked my ass (although once, while I gave him head, he did make a big deal about being so horny he wanted to bend me over and fuck me. But again: he did not).

He was hot, and the illicit energy of our encounters was thrilling, something interesting for me to do while I flushed my education down the drain. Some part of me can't believe that I regularly cut classes at my community college just to touch his dick, driving in the opposite direction to a completely different neighborhood from school just to fuck him. I lied about where I was, when I'd be home. But I felt a kinship with him, an understanding. We were both liars with, apparently, uninhibited sex drives. And it was either suck Plinio's cheater dick or draw polystyrene spheres in a dusty drawing studio. I'd already spent four years being drilled on the elements of art, rendering and painting, and thinking really hard about art, just to end up another aimless, wayward loser in the desert. So yeah, sucking some cheater dick was a marginally more appealing way to pass the time than playing with charcoal.

But even my playtime with Pliny eventually came to an end. I used to be a serious cock slut, eager to blow someone just for the thrill of being near a man who happened to not have his pants on, but it got old. I was chasing a thrill, something to make me feel alive, and when I realized that the mysterious variables had become known—I'd never be in his house while his kids were home, I could only come over while his girlfriend/wife was at work, he was never going to do anything besides sit in his office chair and let me lick his dick—it all became rote. Digging around in a tub of charcoal with some people pursuing elective credits while they finished their Associate's degree in BioMed slowly became much more fun than driving over to this hollow McMansion deep in the burbs. Plus, despite having two kids, Pliny always shot blanks. I'd work on his knob for so long, he'd build up to this orgasm and tell me about how much he was going to cum, and then the smallest, most miniscule pearl of semen would rise up from his slit. I'd pretend like he'd just absolutely drenched me in cum, obviously, for his ego. But it was generally unsatisfying. He had evidently used up all his cum getting girls pregnant and not on showering nineteen-year-old twunks. I decided to end things.

Voracious gay sex is how I waded into girlhood. While you're fucking someone, the edges of your body start to blur and are replaced by feelings of pleasure, stimulation. I felt around for the edges of my gender in the bodies of the men who fucked me.

There was the pilot who flew a private jet for some anonymous millionaire and stayed at the Westgate right off The Strip when he had a layover in the city and his patron wanted to gamble. He'd invite me over so he could penetrate me on all fours while I looked at the skyline through the large window by his hotel bed.

There was also the cycling-obsessed solar panel salesman I'd meet up with at public bathrooms around the outdoor mall by my house so we could have silent, feral intercourse in the stalls. I felt where our bodies looked the same and where they contrasted—the way these dudes carried themselves, so securely in their identity as men, and where we met in between, when they showed me their surprisingly un-macho traits. When big men wanted me to spoon them, or when buff men talked up how masculine I looked (to my surprise), I realized that I wasn't trapped in my body. I could define it for myself.

These Craigslist encounters were exercises in creative writing. I'd write the roles and cast myself and some stranger in them. Maybe this time I was a young Asian femme looking for some fun. Another time I'd be a boy who wants someone to make him feel like a girl. Another time I was an artsy bisexual looking for a threesome. Another time I was tall, beefy, and macho and wanted to find someone even taller, beefier, and macho-er to pin me down. These were all roles I thought about playing, seeing how they felt. Seeing what it felt like to be fucked while wearing that mask. I calibrated my spirit in this way, finding what mask felt good to wear and what mask felt alienating. Which mask felt like me and which felt like a stranger's?

That's the not-so-well-kept secret about gay male sex for would-be-trans girls: you can engage in something that seems like male for male sex, but you can project a new reality using your mind. You can bottom for a big strong man, one who will call you his bitch, talk about breeding you and making you pregnant, and for a while, your naked body will feel like a woman's next to his.

Maybe this is why some people take other people on dates before their NSA sex. It makes things feel cinematic or literary or something when your night starts out inside someone's shiny black sedan or when you're wined and dined at a beautiful restaurant, and you feel like Julia Roberts in *Pretty Woman*, or at the very least like a beautiful pig getting stuffed on acorns before getting slaughtered. I'm talking about a full body experience here—mind and soul. You can, at the very least, pretend that there is something grand at play, that you carry marginally more worth than a Fleshlight. These dudes were decent in the sack, but what I remember most was that they enthralled all of my senses. I didn't get the dates, the tease of a story, but I did get a sort of foreplay. The sex would start before I even met them, with a story on Craigslist. Something like: *I'm a single horny dad in the suburbs and I'm looking for a twink or a crossdresser to satisfy my urge while the wife's away.* It's fun to play a character—who doesn't want to be the slutty crossdressing twink next door when it's a freaking sexy DILF on the line?

I'm a slightly more experienced sex-haver now who doesn't have to sneak away from my dad or cut class to sneak in a fuck. Maybe that's why the regular hookups don't feel as fun as they used to. Like, where are all the easily accessible, horny PILFs[3] who want to cruise at a park and try to guess which men in little running shorts are into me and which of them are just corny dads in tiny running shorts? I want to feel the way I did the first time I felt the pang, that phantom of gender-affirmation when a man calls me "baby" while he's in me. I want to sit pretty in a luxurious bar and be approached by a beautiful woman in a suit and courted gentlemanly like a lady in an Austen novel then get slammed in her bedroom like an episode of *Bridgerton*.

Is it asking too much to find someone who wants to establish a sex-first relationship with me, beyond the calendar-coordinating and dry direct

---

3   Plural form of PILF (Parent I'd like to fuck) which I think works as the gender-neutral version of MILF or DILF.

messages? I want to live in that obsession of mutual desire and affection, where the psychic storm between two minds conjures a lusty fantasy, and every conversation drips with seduction.

Sex doesn't have to begin and end with a kiss and a cum. It can begin at first glance, at *hello!* It's not over when your insides are flooded or when someone screams with pleasure. It can continue into the laughter after the orgasm, into the conversation that you have once your brains are temporarily clear of that hedonistic fog of lust, to dinner and breakfast and lunch. So many people give up before I'm satisfied. Leave it on the couch, in the condom. Always the foreplay, never the after care. It's like these people have never thought about the narrative structure of a good story. I can't truly be a sex addict under these dire conditions. I want more more more more more more more, and I don't want it all to end right in the middle, right when it's getting exciting.

* * *

When I look back, my boyhood was full of self-loathing and confusion. I hated my body and felt like it limited me from everything I wanted to be. It reminded me of where I wasn't allowed to go, who I wasn't allowed to be. What I really miss was not thinking about sex. For most of my time as a trans girl, my sex life has felt complicated. I was in a long term, non-monogamous relationship with my ex for seven years. But I was severely depressed and figuring my shit out, with my hormones, with my early twenties. My libido was up and down, as were my finances, my emotional interiority. It's less that I miss being a boy, I guess, and more that sometimes I miss the simplicity of being a young, voracious slut. When I wasn't so concerned with living or dying, when I could wade into a room of gay men and think, I could fuck anyone in this room. Now, I conduct a little more of a mental sorting process.

I enter a room and think, *Anyone in this room could be a transphobe.* The roles I played during my encounters with men were all set up by me, two dudes on even playing ground acting out a fantasy. Now my fantasy is my real life, I'm a girl 24/7. I live my life as a trans woman, feeling all the complicated feelings of being a woman who wants to fuck people and being a sensitive tranny with an ego that has the fortitude of a house of cards.

And when you're a trans girl, you're not just a girl. A girl can be extremely beautiful and live a quiet life. The kind of quiet life that is impressive; like, Oh you went to Idyllwild with your boyfriend for a week? Your mom makes $500,000 a year and you have a wardrobe made of Alaïa and Paloma Wool and some archival Miu Miu, but you just throw on the Lululemon when you need to run to Trader Joe's. Like, it's no big deal, obviously. Beautiful cis girls can live that sort of life and never be bothered by anyone.

Trans girls become a specific kind of person only liked by specific kinds of people. Okay, like I actually think that most people are neutral-to-positive about trans people, but I'm talking about my feelings here so let me be a bit melodramatic. Yes, for the most part, other humans see me as another human, just some tall, maybe slightly weird-looking human, walking down the street. But there's a faction of people who become obsessed with you, with us—in a different way than the way people are obsessed with gay men. That kind of obsession is like the way you feel when you look at a tiny dog: you want it, you want it to cuddle with you every night, be its best friend, and wear matching outfits to the mall together. The obsession with trans people is more like what happens when an extraterrestrial visitor suddenly appears in the town square. These people want to know you, know what's going on, be near you, figure you out. A few people become obsessed and want to love the alien, maybe without ever really understanding why. Other people find out about this alien, this intruder, and they get mad, like it's a sign from God or something higher or something evil like Satan. They want to kill you, fuck you up.

Or at the very least, they want to fuck you.

This is why I think every trans girl worth her salt should spend some time in Fag World. It's so much fun to fuck men as a man. There's a level of equality in male-dominated spaces. When you get to go into a steamy sex club and see everyone as a potential fuck and are seen by everyone else as a potential fuck, you get to glimpse at an egalitarian sex utopia. Like, obviously yes, it's a utopia built on exclusion, but it's nice to be on the inside. There's kind of a reason homosexual men occupy so much of the gay spaces—especially faggots who spend so much of their life on the outside—it feels good. Sucks to say, but it's true.

Being a trans girl will get you to access so many other spaces that you can never have dreamed of accessing before. These new places will feel just as euphoric as gay male spaces, maybe even more so. Dyke parties, trans families, T4T love. But there's a nostalgia I have for the simple fun of being a dude fucking another dude.

There's a thrill that comes with fucking a near-stranger that's hard to replicate. Even when the actual sex is bad (which it kind of frequently is). As a trans girl, I've still fucked lots of strangers, people I barely knew and probably should have done a better job vetting. But less so. Once you cross over into girlhood you get exposed to more danger (which can be fun), more microaggressions (less fun), and you'll feel a little more sensitive to being treated improperly. Now I kind of want to feel more than just a physical chemistry with the people I fuck. This has really dampened my sluttery, which I'm super bummed about, but has all in all been better for my psyche.

You can see why I lowkey miss the faggotry of all-male cruising spaces. It's a bit simpler, there are less feelings. I've gone whole encounters without speaking more than five sentences, communicated almost entirely in short, imperative statements like stop, that kinda hurts, that feels really good, go faster, and I'm going to cum. The only questions I asked: Do you have roommates? Do you have condoms? Where do you want it?

The rest of the communication happens between our bodies.

* * *

I ideated on femininity for years, never feeling super comfortable within the mold of masculinity and all its trappings. It's not that masculinity is inherently toxic. Like, I love men, I love butches, transmasc babes, proxy father figures. But, as you may well know, the gender binary is strictly enforced across the U.S., and while I think I've always been rather femmey and gay-like, I have also often been among the tallest and heaviest in my class, often one of the bigger people in any room.

Picture me as a fourteen-year-old: chubby face, skin deeply tan from playing in the pool at our apartment complex for hours and hours. Cargo shorts from the "husky" section and a vaguely sporty T-shirt, although I was far from athletic. My thick black hair sat on my head like a Lego figurine's, the same length all the way around, dense and heavy. My eyebrows thick and bushy, always threatening to become one. I never had a growth spurt growing up. I just steadily grew taller and faster than everyone else so that I always stood two or three heads above everyone else. I'd also always carried a little pudge all the way around my body, manifesting usually in a soft belly, flabby chest, and big meaty calves.

As a child, I hated being tall, mostly because I preferred to blend in. Being noticed often meant some sort of comment about my body was going to be lobbed my way: I was chubby, I should play basketball, I was handsome. Relatively neutral comments to hear as a child, but to me they always reminded me of where I fell short. Tall but horrible at basketball. I never fit in with the boys, never understood the language of masculinity. It always seemed to be about being just the right amount of boisterous, knowing when to laugh and when to razz someone else. It meant not only being good at sports but wanting to play them all the time. I was easily overwhelmed as a child, vaguely asthmatic and fighting a chronic stomach issue. I was a fucking dweeb, and I did not want to throw a ball around and run until my breath became sharp and ragged, until my stomach hurt and I had to run to the bathroom. I wanted to be safe inside, away from people who projected ideas of who I was onto me and were vaguely disappointed that this tall beefy kid did not want to use his body to score points.

* * *

I'd spent my entire life failing at boyhood, never making friends or joining sports teams, not really doing anything that any child should be spending their time doing. My family moved several times between the Bay Area and Las Vegas, and even once we settled in Las Vegas we often moved clear across town into an entirely new neighborhood and school system. I didn't make any friends that lasted. By the time I was in 8th grade, I'd found my niche in a small friend group of intense, nerdy girls where I felt vaguely allowed to be a little more myself. With these girls I was just some gay boy, invited to sleepovers and playing video games all day after school, thinking about grades and messing around on the internet.

The first time I was allowed to pick my own set of clothes rather than wear what my parents bought for me, I gravitated towards a pink button up shirt in the men's section. It was a frat boy button up shirt more than anything, but it was the safest taste of material femininity that I could attempt to hold. Even then, the cashier gave me some grief: Oh yeah, pink's not just for girls anymore! Which of course only reminded me of how much I was being perceived as a boy, a non-girl-shaped human made to feel ashamed and embarrassed.

I at least had the luck of winning a lottery to get into an arts magnet school, the only one in the city at the time. This stroke of luck protected me from going to my local public school, where I *might* have survived, but considering I nearly dropped out of my 75% female, relatively queer-friendly arts high school and still frequently ideated about suicide, I'm not sure I would have gotten out with my life and/or diploma.

Anyway, at this arts magnet school I was surrounded by mostly intense, art-obsessed girls of all kinds. I'm not sure what the state of the Clark County school district is these days (probably not great), but back then it was the only school for visual and performing arts where students could focus on their disciplines for at least two hours every day and were expected to keep up with a rigorous academic regimen as well. This was the school you went to if you were: too poor to go to a private school, not STEM-oriented enough to go to a technical school, and masochistic enough to commute to downtown Las Vegas from whatever suburb you lived in every day, for four years.

Here, in this social experiment with questionable morals, where teens are pushed to their absolute limit, I became increasingly faggy and really didn't have to worry about getting bullied or beat up or anything. In fact, I think the faggier and weirder I got, the more social currency I had.

By the time I was a senior, I'd shed my husky cargo shorts and oversized T-shirts for a pastel goth aesthetic. My favorite outfit was baby blue overalls cut into short shorts, a turquoise and lavender striped polo T-shirt and four-inch tall platform creepers—turning me into a 6'4" gay behemoth that *owned* my shit. I cut my hair into an extreme undercut so that my skull was bared all way around my head save for a crown of increasingly long, bleach blond curls. I was living my fag truth!

At this point, I'd honestly shed any notions of living out some boyhood and chose to live instead in this in-between space that I didn't have the language for. This was before I, or most people, knew about the word nonbinary. I'd read of identities like genderfuck and genderfluid on Tumblr, but even those phrases felt a little fringe. Then there was the increasingly popular transgender label and the more popular labels: transvestite, transsexual—both of which felt a little too extreme for my pre-transition, egg[4] vibes.

When I was seventeen or eighteen years old, there were several times when I yelled, "I'm not a boy!" at some innocuous proclamation of gender. For instance, boys and girls would be separated into different areas by some authority figure, and instead of compliance I'd overtly protest, annoyingly, leave the room entirely, or side with girls. One of my good friends, Sol, was also proto-nonbinary, and we would often slide together as partners, an unspoken understanding between gender nonconforming friends. This unspoken partnership increased in volume—Sol and I understood each other on lots of levels. Like me, they were an adultified kid, *paying rent* to their parents since they were sixteen, translating documents for their Colombian

---

4   Someone who does not realize they're trans yet. It's obvious to anyone else who has transitioned but not to the egg. IE: An egg that is about to hatch. You're not allowed to use this term unless you're trans.

parents, working jobs after school, messing around with drugs and sexual partners of questionable quality. The two of us were, in short, raw dogging life A process that alienated us from our peers, who seemed for the most part to be living more conventionally juvenile lifestyles. So, there we were, two not-boys not-girls, dealing with our intense, vampiric families with jobs, grappling with our art practices and school. Two tired gender-weird souls. At one point we came to school in our matching genderfag uniform: platform shoes and cut-off overalls. I mean, how else do you protest gender norms and protest everything you hate in the world? With style, babe.

Looking back, I see so many of these actions, these ways that I refused to fit in, and I see several attempts to abandon manhood, slowly leaving the house that my father built for me. That was how I left behind my boyhood, but it wasn't until I started having lots of gay sex with men that I started my proper foray into girlhood.

PASSING IS A DANGEROUS GAME

A couple of days after the Prince and I broke up, I fucked a bouncer at my favorite bar in a dark alley down the street. The divorce, initially very amicable, had boiled over. Years of bottled-up fights poured out all at once, fumigating the apartment. I spent a lot of this time holed up in the office—my bedroom since the breakup. But, missing the warmth of Chicago summer, I put on my new tennis dress, a white athletic little garment with a built-in sports bra and skort. I decided to leave my sad little breakup hovel. I didn't want to witness my roommate's sweet honeymoon era with her new boyfriend, I didn't want to bark barely civil sentences at my ex, I didn't want to hear them all laughing together in the living room, all of them not hormonal and sad and me both of those things. I shoved a pile of books and my Nintendo Switch into my bag and went outside to be avoidant—but, at least be avoidant in the sunshine.

A dress is all about the cut. Sometimes a short dress like this makes me feel like an awkward wedge of a human, a fashion newbie who's playing dress up in their sister's clothes. It brings up feelings of fraudulence and dysphoria. That day, though? No. The dress felt light and airy. The built-in sports bra flattened my already very tiny boobs, but the high-cut skirt showed off my long, muscular legs.

At my favorite bar down the street, I ordered a tall glass of Old Style and drank it really slowly so I could loiter without feeling too guilty about it. I was never someone who lingers in bars alone, but it felt very in-character for me, as a divorcée, to be drowning my feelings in some beer. After about three hours of reading and idly playing video games, stretching my drink out for as long as possible, I decided to suck it up, be brave enough to step through my avoidant feelings and walk back to my apartment where my ex and my roommate were likely chumming it up in the living room, right in front of the door.

Half-way down the block, someone tapped me on the shoulder. I looked up to see the bouncer from the bar. I was confused—had I forgotten my wallet? My book? He said that he got cut from his shift early and asked if I wanted a drink. He'd called out to me while I walked away, but my headphones drowned out sound. In the amber streetlight, I took a good look at him—as best I could without my glasses that I'd shorn in vanity—and quickly realized: I was looking up at him. He was tall. He was wide. He had long locs that dangled around his shoulders and a cute face hidden behind golden glasses. Yeah, I could be down for another drink. Bouncer's got a name: Curly.

I returned to the bar and said hello to the bartender I just said goodbye to. Bartender gave me a friendly smile and tried to conceal a knowing look to me and Curly. In exchange for the minor humiliation, some complimentary shots—two shots of Malört for Curly and Bartender, a shot of tequila for me. We talked about our lives: his stint in the military, his two degrees. Two. His daughter, whom he loves. His parents. I mentioned my burgeoning career in media, my recent breakup, and did not bring up the college degree I do not have.

A couple of bars later, a couple of shots later, he asked me in a low tone: "What's up?" Like, *what's up* what's up. The kind of what's up that means, where do we go from here? Followed up by the more explicit: "Whatchu trying to do?" I? I was trying to fuck.

After a sloppy make out at the second (or third?) bar, he asked me where I live. I laughed and told him that where I live is down the street, and where I live contained my ex and an abundance of weird, fresh breakup vibes.

I didn't want to come stumbling through the living room with this big, manly rebound.

"Where do you live?" I asked and he told me he lives with his teenage daughter, who he does not want to fuck up by bringing home a stranger to have loud, drunk sex with. We agreed on two things: we want more, and we cannot take each other home. The location for where *more* will happen was yet to be determined, but that would not stop us.

I got in his Charger and luxuriated in the space. The first car in years I could really stretch out in, where my knees didn't touch the dash and fold awkwardly under my body. It was clean. It smelled nice. I pet the leather seats while he started the car and felt a charge rise through my body. I'm a pretty girl who got picked up, and I'm in a Charger. In all my years of sluttery, I have never been picked up in real life. I've had strange sex in bathhouses, I've had plenty of hookups aided by Craigslist and Grindr, but not the kind of hookup I see on TV, where people meet in the club and follow each other to a second location. It was hot and affirming. Who knew all I had to do was sit in a bar in a short skirt and read books?

In the blurry, drunken darkness of the night we found an alley behind some greystones and tucked into an alcove built into a brick wall, intended to house trash. After moving the trash bins around so that we could hide, I blew him. My mouth wet with spit, I pulled back from his dick and asked him to fuck me.

While we thrusted quietly in this trash alley, nothing but the sound of flesh clapping together and our hushed breaths, he reached around to my crotch —but then quickly backed off. I realized that I haven't exactly disclosed.

Does he know I'm trans?

* * *

I've never really strived to pass as a cis woman. It was always going to be a losing game for me, six feet tall, deep voice. No matter how pretty I made myself, my skeleton wouldn't change. And I was much too lazy to modulate my voice with voice training. Listen, I care deeply about beauty and pampering and my self-image, but I've always wanted to build an otherworldly beauty. I've never wanted to be regular-degular. Sure, I don't love being seen as a man in makeup when I'm out and about, or hear a cashier say, "Thank you, sir" when I go and order McDonald's for lunch. But I don't want to blend in. I want to be worshiped. When I sit in front of the mirror to do my makeup, I channel elven princesses, goddesses, pop divas, and drag queens. I don't look like a cis woman.

I look better.

From my tract house in the desert, a larval fag in the years before chrysalis, I watched a lot of YouTube videos. Videos of drag queens prancing around in the dark of the night, the light from an iPhone flash illuminating their faces painted with glamourous shellac an inch thick. The cackling, the walking, the passersby showering them with stares and praise, cars driving by and honking. They had power.

I watched archival videos of Cher in bespoke Bob Mackie garments, doing crowd work and dancing across the stage with her enviously huge hair. I lingered on gifsets of Cher that got reblogged onto my dashboard back when everyone was on Tumblr. People dedicated digital altars—entire blogs and websites—to Cher's glamour. She commanded attention for decades because of her talent, but also because of her distinct look. Who the hell else looks like Cher?

Beauty gurus uploaded get-ready-with-me videos, transforming themselves from regular, symmetrical, pretty girls—with some normal discoloration and perhaps visible eyebags—into impossible icons of beauty. Their eyes three different colors, their cheeks flushed and glowing, lips immaculately painted on. They were not just women wearing makeup, they were something else. Walking art. Witches. Their ability to transform earned them corporate sponsored trips to remote locations, free clothes, hundreds of thousands of devoted fans, and money. It gave them power. Power to leave their humble beginnings in small towns across America. It gave them the freedom to quit whatever day jobs they were working, whatever career path they were building with their college degree. Now they could have fun. These are deities *above* human beings. They had agency, power, and glamour. They were twinkly and shiny and looked like walking illustrations, sculptures—art. I wanted to be like that.

* * *

When I was eighteen, my art class took a field trip to San Francisco. I'd been playing with gender fuckery for a while by then–I had an extreme undercut all the way around my head, and my bleach-blond curls dangled from the crown of my skull down to my jaw. My uniform was strictly pastel goth, little hoochie daddy running shorts, mint-colored tank tops and Polos, transparent PVC accessories with pink pleather straps. I loved to wear over-the-knee socks with my four-inch platform creepers. I was a twunky teenager with pretty Asian genes, well on my way out of the Man-Land. The concept of being nonbinary wasn't as widespread as it is now, so I didn't have the language to explain what the hell I was doing. Instead, I'd just yell *I'm not a boy!* anytime my classmates and I were organized into gender for crowd control. Once, a teacher, fed up with my insubordination, shot back, "So, are you a girl?" I didn't really feel like a girl at the time, but I knew I was something else. Definitely not a boy. I knew I was a fag. Maybe I was a monster.

Being the only non-girl on that interstate trip meant I got quartered in my own hotel room while everyone else was doubled or tripled up. This was the result of my failure to pass, of being seen as not-a-girl. Perhaps it is relentless optimism, or thick skin, but I didn't feel like an alienated freak, quarantined in a room. I felt like a diva. Like, you cis bitches *wish* you could have your own room.

* * *

After I'd publicly declared my transition, I became preoccupied with performing a high-femme persona at all times, partly because it felt euphoric to be so unapologetically girly after a lifetime of only dabbling in flamboyance. I wouldn't even walk to the grocery store—literally a three minute walk from my apartment—without full coverage foundation, light contouring and strobing, eyeliner, a subtle cut-crease and lip gloss. Now that I was a trans girl, I didn't want to be caught outside looking like a boy. It somehow felt fraudulent—both as to how I wanted to present myself to the world and to this new me that I'd debuted to society.

After starting estrogen, my body started to change too. Before, I could turn on anonymous boy mode—baggy sweatpants, a big sweater, a hat, and a surgical mask. Become this androgynous blob, probably a stinky boy, but not anyone you'd think twice about passing on the street. The estrogen worked slowly, so I helped it along where I could: shaving my brows so I could draw cunty little arched lines instead. But this meant going out in boy mode made me look not like a boy, but a daywalker[5]. I'd grown little tender boobs, and the fat on my body had ever so slightly started to shift into an hourglass shape. That secret trans girl signal had turned the volume up. I couldn't suppress it as easily under boy clothes. I was, in short, clocky.

* * *

When I first started having sex, I played up a pretty-baby, fag persona. My Craigslist ads would mention my inexperience, my eagerness to learn how to blow someone or take a cock up my ass. I'd mention my age, tender and eighteen, so that I'd feel like an ingenue, the young hot thing from next door. The men I'd fuck could feel like big, manly bulls taking in their quarry. I'd learned early on that contrast was an easy way to mess with gender.

A lot of us transition, of course, to be seen and desired a certain way by others. The kinds of people I fucked or was interested in didn't really change, but I felt like they could at least see me the way I wanted to be seen. That gap between how I felt in my mind's eye, in my fantasy, and how I was actually seen was a deep, deep chasm. When the dream world and material world don't align, it's devastating.

Being a little gay boy, a pre-transition girl, when the people you have crushes on don't see you and want you in the way that feels right, its alienating. I think that's what doctors like to call dysphoria. Medical shorthand to describe a mangled knot of dark feelings. I didn't want to be a man in a relationship with a womanplaying up all the parts of myself I didn't like, exactly how masculine I was—tall, broad, short hair—and exactly how masculine I wasn't—queer, undercut, artsy, weird. It brought up all the

---

5   A prostitute in the daytime. A drag queen in the daytime.

ways I felt inadequate my whole life. I understood my attraction to boys—a femme gay guy who just liked dudes. There was less room for all my insecurity. But all the boys I were into wanted to be with more masculine men, or with women. I think part of myself wanted to transition into something more likeable by all the people I'd been chasing my whole life.

But getting obsessed with passing is a dangerous path to go down. It's the same trap that cis women are compelled into: the performance of gender, the pink tax. Not just with the extra creams and razors and treatments, but in the time and energy required to be in public. The work required to go outside. If cis women feel this much pressure to perform the gender they were assigned at birth, trans women feel doubly so. It's an obstacle that sometimes keeps you trapped in the house, fearful of going outside looking like a *monster.* Or worse, the palpability of this pressure to perform may stop you from transitioning at all.

I won't deny that when I walk outside the house, I am making calculated choices about just how weird, how clocky, how visible I want to be. But for the most part, I try to cultivate a transfemme beauty. When I go to a drag show, I see so much of it, and it fills me with a warm, tingling sense of safety. Walking into a dark club lit up by the glitter of twinks and dolls and queens and dykes, their shiny skin, their satin dresses. Immaculate makeup and a big bushy beard, a prominent Adam's apple and a floor-length gown, a big, visible dick bulging against a tight miniskirt. It's fuckin' hot, babe. But it doesn't just have to be in the club! I love signaling that I'm trans. I mean, how stealth could I really be, a giant Filipino woman in the Midwest with curly red hair? But I love to make it obvious that I'm a trans girl—a femme with a dick and a deep voice. My eyeliner, my "I'm clearly trans" choker, my little lab-grown tits, I wear them all with pride. And, perhaps, as armor. It's aposematism, my warning color. Do not approach unless you want to talk to a tranny.

I've always felt like life was more dangerous when I looked stealth, anyway. I used to walk around my neighborhood in Vegas looking relatively stealth, maybe more like a cis streetwalker than anything, and found myself having to deal with aggressive men (aggressive men who may or may not have come to terms with any latent queerness, or transamorous feelings). I could tell when someone was thirsting after me in a "you think I'm a cis girl" way, and I'd have to diffuse the situation without clocking myself, saying "no thanks, have a nice day," with a heavy voice that dropped like a brick. Trans panic is a fucking bullshit excuse for defense, but it also defines a phenomenon: unhealed men who feel surprised that they are attracted to a girl with a dick. That sort of shit can get you hurt. No thanks. I prefer to just look like a weird, nonbinary fag with a very pretty face. That way, if someone wants to hurt me, they'll just throw a brick from afar, or yell a slur or something.

Passing does have a role as a tool, I won't deny that. It can smooth over the turbulence of day-to-day life as a trans girl; it did for me. Even if I wasn't always passing-passing, cashiers would at least see the eyeliner and the skirt and say, "Thank you, ma'am," instead of "Thank you, sir." I did get sir'd, just less often. But for most of us, passing isn't just a dangerous game, it's a losing one. The barometer for what qualifies as a cis woman changes with every person, in every city, with every year. If you were a lady who wore pants in the 1930s, you were basically a heathen. Some cis women, not a queer bone in their body, wouldn't pass the test for passing as cis because of the shape of their head or the cut of their hair. Predicating my safety on this constant, high-level performance of cis-femininity was not the fucking vibe. I knew that it was always an illusion of safety, one that could be shattered any minute. And for me, it's also predicated on looking like a brown woman—a class of person whose safety has never been guaranteed anywhere on this planet.

Threading the needle between pretty and unremarkably feminine can get you through a bus or train ride without being hassled, might prevent you from getting misgendered when you order some food at the takeout counter, might save a bit of that emotional pain and dysphoric spiraling. But remember, beauty is a tool—you can use it to bring yourself closer to a heavenly alien creature, paint a picture of the kind of person you want to be, use it to scare away predators—or like camouflage to get through the day. Don't worship the tool, don't worship the beauty. Worship the truth and pleasure and getting a kick out of people staring.

Passing is dangerous because it locks you into patriarchal ideas of beauty. You've gone through all this trouble to transition, to live your full life, only to find yourself locked into the binaristic jail of gender. You realize that the other side of the bars is also a jail.

I've always liked people who look like cartoon characters, who have distinct looks injected with tons of personal style and idiosyncrasies. Some unsolicited advice from me: I don't think anyone should concern themselves with passing. Don't pass—create. Build. Paint. Don't be a pretty girl, be an alien princess who has fallen to earth and needs to get groceries. Be the goth girl in the back of the class who is really good at crocheting. Be a lady jock with huge biceps and formfitting athletic wear on at all times. Personally, I like to cultivate a sort of prep-at-an-all-girls-Christian-school-who-carries-an-evil-secret-and-practices-witchcraft-on-the-weekend vibe. It's so much more fun and liberating to create new worlds and new identities, to project. To cultivate a beauty that's not concerned with safety or appeasing others, but instead with casting glamour spells and imagining a whole new world.

* * *

The morning after my post-breakup romp in a trash alley, I texted Curly. We flirted and discussed the fun we had. I brought up the hesitation I felt around my crotch. I asked if he knew I was trans and if that was cool with him. He told me he knew what was up and what he was doing, but that *Some of the girls don't love having their dick touched because it makes them feel dysphoric.* He wasn't being a weirdo, and he wasn't surprised by my cock. He was just being as smooth as he could, given the circumstances—mid-coitus, drunk in a dumpster alley with a stranger at midnight. I didn't pass. I was a hot trans lady, and he wanted some.

NO POWER, NO SAFETY

One of the tools of survival for a trans girl is passing. At least, that is what they say. You can trade in all the power that being an unapologetically, beautifully *clockable* trans woman gives you for the ability to go incognito.

Personally, my transition was motivated by an obsession with *stars*—shiny people who oozed charisma, the kind of people that turn heads and command cameras and draw crowds with their mere presence. My role models were drag queens, pop stars, and gold diggers. I did not ever aspire to *blend in.* Throughout my girlhood, there have definitely been times when I was a bit more concerned with passing, spurred on possibly by whatever was the most recent murder of a trans woman at the time. My anxiety about being killed in public stacked up with the general insecurity of being in my early twenties and often resulted in heavy makeup, painstakingly painted to re-sculpt my face and turn the bigger parts smaller, the smaller parts bigger. Besides those blips of judgment, I don't really understand the obsession with being a normal girl, of dedicating your entire life, so much money, to this every-woman thing, the most generic woman possible—beautiful, but not so much as to draw attention, turning your outie into an innie just so that your future husband won't be able to tell you were born with something a little extra. Don't get me wrong, I'm in favor of the dolls getting as much plastic surgery as they possibly can, milking pay pigs and sugar daddies and governmental assisted surgery funds for all they got so they can go under the knife, but only for one's own self-satisfaction. The idea that one day, you'll cross the threshold and become so passable that you're elevated to this other place that marks you safe from gunmen and capitalists and violent transphobes of all kinds feels like a false mirage.

There have been a few times both online and in real life where I (of all people!) have been mistaken for a cis woman, only to surprise people with my voice, or my dick, or the blatant proclamation of loving my transness, but even then I never felt like I was safe. Even if I did look like a cis woman—I've got brown skin. In that case, I'm not a trans woman but a fat brown lady, or maybe some kind of dyke. Was I really so much safer in those moments? What woman of color do you know that feels completely safe walking down the street?

FREEDOM IS BETTER THAN FAME IS BETTER THAN MONEY

In the pockets of my Stealing Jacket were a tomato and a small red onion. I paid for the fried fish, the unctuous smell seeping through its paper wrapping, and a bundle of fragrant cilantro which was sixty-nine cents. Pompano, my favorite fish, is cheap and delicious, its flavor unfurling like a bouquet in your mouth. At 99 Ranch you can get them to clean and fry your fish at no extra cost, and I will do anything if there is no extra cost. At home, we steamed a pot of rice so that my partner and my sister and I could feast Kamayan style on this bounty, less than $10 for all three of us to get full. My own willpower amazed me. I was hungry and broke, stringing together rent for our apartment on a block I once heard someone refer to as "opium alley." I liked that block. I think it got a bad rap, it was no more dystopian or horrible than any other block in Vegas. My building was full of people like me, lots of hot trans girls and strippers walking home in their short skirts and pink dresses and heels, maybe coming home from a trick or a party or their office job. Older folks, maybe living off their retirements or their part-time office jobs. Parents, families. There were a lot of us crammed into that old building, plus a herd of rats that liked to run laps in our vents, a small colony of cockroaches, some houseless people who'd walk in off the street and take shelter in our stairwells. We all got along well. Sometimes, there would be a fight in the hall, a spat between a couple, resulting in furniture being haphazardly thrown out of an apartment. Sometimes, there would be a gunshot, sometimes a misunderstanding or a beef escalated too far, and sometimes a scream. Sometimes a death. For the most part, we all got along.

I think about money a lot—I can't help it. I'm an Earth sign. But I despise capitalism, the slow commodification of everything into its monetary value, the flattening of people, time, animals, plants, of everything in existence. All the molecules in the universe weighed and measured in exact currency, to be exchanged for something—I don't know what. Maybe it's not money that I like, but a sense of security that I find comfort in. Material happiness, cozy creature comforts. Money buys that.

At some point in my early twenties, I started a GoFundMe. My guile and cunning had run out—too many bills, too little income from my day job. My side hustle which consisted primarily of hanging out with creepy tourists on Grindr for money and writing SEO-friendly clickbait about my #TransgenderBeautyRoutine helped me make ends meet in the months before, but now all of that had gone dry. My laptop, a workhorse I'd relied on for years, suddenly gave out on me. I opened it one day and the screen slowly turned black like an old tube TV, and then refused to turn on again. Uh-oh. A laptop feels like a luxurious thing to fret about, but my computer is how I made money—it's how I planned to make *more* money. It's how I lived my life. And now it was not working. I had to become a beggar and do all of this on someone else's laptop.

Luckily, I'd spent most of my life advertising myself on Craigslist for hookups, writing content that would catch eyes on the internet. I knew how to package myself to be consumed. In this case I needed to be a beautiful yet down on my luck trans girl of color. Help me! I'm trying so hard! It was true, but humiliating to put on this performance of suffering so that I could not be suffering anymore. I felt like a busker, but instead of dancing or singing, I was a clown, performing transgender poverty, a vessel to receive money and aid so that someone else could feel better about themselves.

* * *

An Instagram infographic recently told me to STOP MENTAL MASTURBATION. I feel like I'm doing that all the time, and now an Instagram user with Canva told me to stop, so I probably should. According to them, mental masturbation is the act of "artificially" raising your dopamine levels by telling people your plans for a new project or new self-improvement goal and never following up on said plans. Your brain, already satisfied by the positive stimuli, does not want to work to enact whatever it is you were planning to do—write a book, start a new exercise regimen, go vegan.

I don't really do this kind of mental masturbation anymore. But, I definitely discussed ideas for new projects with friends and strangers before I really got going, only to lose steam before I finished anything. Now I can kind of trick my ADHD-addled brain, so starved for dopamine, into doing work before I give it candy. While this results in a productive life, I find it hard to keep my brain satisfied. It hates working for days, weeks, months without gratification, and it's desperate for positive stimuli. I need fireworks, candy, bass booming on the dance floor, and strangers rubbing against me.

I've been on a Mindful Separation from dating and hookup apps. No Grindr, Sniffies, Craigslist, Feeld, Hinge, Tinder, Pinder, Kinder, Lesbians4Now.com, or TrannyDate on my phone.

A bad habit of browsing Grindr for hours like a little rat pushing a button over and over again even if it electrocuted me without giving me candy, combined with a series of bad hookups, prompted me to consider an app-cleanse. Maybe I should stop pressing the button. Being a kinda-hot trans girl on The Apps is borderline-hazardous for any doll with a dopamine-desperate brain. We[6] are popular on The Apps, but somehow,

---

6   The girls, the dolls, the femmeboys. We! Us.

simultaneously, an acquired taste, like caviar or foie gras. Not everyone is sophisticated enough to appreciate our beauty. Especially compared to a more mainstream, perhaps more *palatable* aesthetic like, say, a white guy with a furry chest and abs, or if you're on The Apps that don't cater to fags and their kin, a pretty cis girl with a round forehead.

The responses you *do* get, however, range from adoration to obsession, fluctuating between idolatry and vitriol. Before my dating hiatus, I regularly received extreme sexual responses with an undercurrent of obsession. The term "love bomb" comes to mind. But you see, transes have fragile egos, like a houses of cards. Or at least, *this* trans does. If we're being real, *that* felt like mental masturbation. But unlike masturbation, this whole game of going hunting for affirmation and/or dick on my phone was a total waste of time. It ultimately did not feel good for my brain to open an app and receive that kind of feedback minute-to-minute, hour-to-hour, day-to-day, week-to-week. Receiving mass feedback—positive and negative—affirmed me, made me feel like I mattered. People hated me, people loved me—there was a reason that I was alive. But even in the other case, where I'd hook someone's attention for a while, ready to drain their energy and love like an IV, and things would not really pan out. Whenever sexting with a rando reached its apex and it was time to plan an IRL hookup, my loins would cool off, the steamy machine of my heart suddenly gone cold and the rosy tinted haze suddenly clear. I don't want to see this loser IRL! During the aforementioned streak of bad hookups, I found myself with the tables reversed on the other end of a one-sided energetic exchange. That is to say: these men were lazy fuckers. There are definitely times when I can get off on giving someone head, but if I expect a little mutual head or some sort of psychic gratification with a *Good girl!* and instead leave with only a sore jaw and the taste of dank testicles on my tongue, I feel a *little* unsatisfied. As you can imagine.

But, then there might be a span of sixty seconds where I don't receive a message of extreme hate/love, and I'd suddenly be a ghost—someone who did not matter, someone who might deserve to die. Some days there would be no one online, or at least no one interested, and that's when I'd fall from grace. No longer a goddess in the heavens worshiped by chasers and bisexuals, but instead a humble, ugly brick hurtling towards Earth.

This sort of rollercoaster, the down and up and down again, while admittedly fun, was rather exhausting. I noticed startlingly similar patterns between myself and those who are addicted to hard substances. I don't want to compare my sad desperate brain to a real struggle with addiction, but if books and movies and other media that are supposed to teach you empathy with others rings true at all, my guess is that love and painkillers and alcohol are all pretty similar. So I quit cold turkey.

The problem now is that I miss mental masturbation, that psychic back and forth, the constant push and pull of my heart's tides felt so good. Physical masturbation is pretty important to my overall health and wellness, and I can't imagine going months without it—so what about mental masturbation? Am I going to have to join a convent? Without The Apps, my fragile transgender psyche is now forced to keep itself fed without the buffet of matches with hot and not so hot people. It's hunting down morsels of dopamine from wherever they can be found. I have spent a good amount of time in real life searching for the lingering gazes of strangers who think I'm beautiful, grasping for a flirtatious energy in a conversation with a rando, trying to psychically instigate sexual encounters with friends-of-friends. The despo meter is high. Not cute, I know.

I live for the attention, though. That visibility makes me feel like I *exist*. That I'm here. So much of my life has felt ghostly, apparition-like. Half here, half in my own imagination. No money or resources to make my dreams real, to make my life real. Every home tenuous, every T-shirt or sock or shoe a luxury. Every good meal feels like it may be my last before I'm back to making and eating calorically maximized slop out of rice or grains or tofu or whatever happens to cost $1. To be seen as a trans girl, to be fucking adored and sought after and fetishized by these random people on the apps, it transformed me from a ghost to a god, from a nobody to a fucking somebody. I sucked it all in. But the thing about gods and ghosts is that neither of them are really human. And, I suppose, I have to be one of those.

$$$

I've spent a lot of my adult life around money. Near it, but never actually *that* close to it, never close enough to grab onto it with my grubby little paws. My proximity and general desperation have generated disgusting amounts of money for people who were already rich. I made a few precious dimes where they've made hundreds. I've always known that this whole capitalism thing was rigged against me. At some point very early on, before the GoFundMe and the psychic fireworks of Grindr and all of that, I'd given up on the fantasy of being rich. I let go of the wish all of us poors like to wish: a jackpot, the lottery, a bank error in my favor. It was never going to happen. And even if I did, somehow, happen upon a fat envelope of cash in the street—then what? How long would it last? Maybe, *maybe*, that nest egg would be enough to keep me safe from instability, from scarcity, to insulate me from the horrors of medical bills and hunger for a while, but would it be enough to protect my friends? My family? Other trans people? Anyone else in the world from any of that? And, if I am a human with an ounce of empathy, how could I feel truly safe and happy knowing that my fortune is not enough to protect anyone else from destitution? I never understood money, but what I did understand was that dollar bills were tokens of power. The more power you had, the greater your ability to make more, the more crime you could get away with, the further away from a normal human you became. The millionaires I've worked for—millionaire sons of millionaire dads of millionaire grandpas—all moved with a cold calculation about human life. They'd gotten so good at reducing humans to their monetary value, their eyes turning people into currency and then taking that currency to make more, leaving behind the shriveled human husks wherever they went. I did not want to be a millionaire making millionaire babies making millionaire grandbabies.

Power, though. It's hard not to get a taste for it. Because I spent so much of my life restricted in my own agency, any drop of freedom feels like manna. I'd do anything for a little more, to quench the desert in my spirit. I know several trans girls, drag queens, and idiosyncratic femmes who have a slightly concerning thirst for power. Most of us quickly grasp onto the idea that power is fungible. Even if you're not born with much of it there are ways to get some, steal it for a second, wield it for your own gain, if not for a fleeting moment of emotional satisfaction. When a drag queen is on stage, she's the motherfucker in charge. Ever had a sparkly drag queen, beautiful and larger than life, yell at you? Command you to throw dollar bills, command you to shut up? Everyone in the club is listening to her, she's got them in her finger tips. Throw some dude up there on the mic and all the queers are definitely not listening, no matter how fat his pockets are. Maybe, if he's hot, heads will turn but no one really gives a fuck. Put the mic back in the shiny drag queen's hand! That's power. I know plenty of trans criminals who commit petty theft to steal back a bit of their power, the agency ripped from them at every stage of their life. Yoink! Dinner. Yoink! Sexy dress. Yoink!

I like to think that, because so many of Us have felt the contours of rock bottom, been left completely disempowered, rendered useless and speechless in the face of giant political machines that want us to die slowly and quietly, en masse, that we really know what it's like to wield power. When we get the spotlight on us, when we have a bit of money, when we have the opportunity to change our reality, we fucking use it, we wield it like a knife.

Maybe fame could protect me from destitution, from becoming dust and forgotten, I think, again and again, in several of my bottom-barrel apartments. Maybe, if I could convince a large enough group of people to love me, they'd all protect me from the evils of bigots, they'd swoop in with another fundraiser if I got attacked or if my house burned down or some other disaster derailed my life.

Well, maybe I can't get famous anytime soon, but at least I could build a local community, I thought. I could build up all this social currency and clout, become famous enough, loved enough by my community, that I'd have that welfare net to protect me from being crushed under a car while sleeping on the streets. I love people, I fucking *love* people, but a part of me felt like, if I help this person to move out of their apartment, or with their project, or bring them some food, then maybe they'd scratch my back when I need it. Maybe not. And I've found the magic of that community, the multiplication of love in mutual aid, how caring about someone else and them caring about me, is not like passing a dollar back and forth, but creating money out of thin air, creating comfort and safety out of pure willpower.

But I know it's not enough. I know that the capitalist death machine is large and powerful and bloodthirsty. I know that we can protect each other from falling to the wayside, from being forgotten or going hungry, from being eaten up, chewed and grinded into nothing by the cogs of it all, but we can only do so much when we're all dealing with medical debt or student loans, or we're all sick or we're all hungry, and our cars are out of gas and all of our money is being leeched to build missiles and shoot them at other poor people halfway across the world. I know now that all of that—the fame and the money and the attention—can keep you out of the death machine's grasp for a little bit, but it is not true freedom. It can't be.

It's all a bit utopian, dreamy maybe, the vision I have for the world. But I've felt it, seen glimpses when I'm having dinner with a friend and I brought the soup and they brought the bread and someone else brought a bottle of wine. None of those things were really a meal, but altogether it's a feast and we're laughing and shining. I've seen it when I've pushed a 500+ pound couch up to the second floor of my friends' apartment, and they fire-lined all my possessions up to the third floor of mine. I've felt it in the surprise gift of flowers, of art, of candy given and received, in a post card out of the blue, in a random phone call, in those magic connections that make the universe feel like it's worth living in. Maybe it's all a bit naïve to think we could have that, more of that, for everyone, but it's something I have to believe is possible. At some point, maybe in my lifetime, or in the life of some trans girl alive several generations after I've died, we have to have built something better, grown something better. I love how it feels to have attention rained down on me—it makes me feel alive—but it's not going to fill my belly. I'm wishing, hoping, dreaming, and working for a world where a girl doesn't have to get on stage and collect attention, love, and praise, try to hold it in her hands like water and alchemize it into food. I want a world where eating and shelter are not even questions, where it's harder to stumble down into the margins and gutters of the world. Where the only question we have to ask is not, "How am I going to eat?" but "How would I like to live?"

HUSTLE KILLS THE GRIND

A couple hours after booking my flight to Seattle, I slid into her DMs on Twitter. I had seen her in the periphery of my internet life, the same way you might see the same person at all the parties in the scene but never actually talk. She'd gotten chummy with cool artist people I followed, chatting about art and obscure vintage video game hardware. I didn't realize I was attracted to her when I sent that message. I just knew I wanted to know her.

I sent the message and promptly began stalking her Tumblr #archive and let the posts wash over me, staring at my screen like it was a Rothko of her interiority. Deep mossy greens, turquoise-y blues, old Japanese geek magazines, an extremely modified GameCube. I tabbed to her selfies and scrolled. A boyish fluffy bowl cut dyed neon green then faded like dry grass. Crash of ocean blue hair on dark fuzzy eyebrows and droopy eyes, skin pale and radiant like a vampire. She looked like a prince. I knew I wanted to know her.

I'd been churning out content for my writing job—if you could even call what I was doing writing. I spent my weeks generating internet drivel for a stunted Rich Boy's clickbait empire, list-style videos that counted down the top ten biggest trees starting from the least biggest down to the biggest of the big. I'd copy-paste some paragraphs about the most dangerous stunts ever performed in motocross history and change a few sentences, scroll through Wikipedia and children's science websites to write lists about the most venomous animals that have *ever* existed. I don't know why, but these videos accrued millions of views—and there were a dozen of us churning them out, altogether generating a billion or so views for my Rich Boy Boss, making him even richer. Rich Boy fancied himself a hippie playboy millionaire, an aspiring bohemian Hugh Hefner—at least according to his SeekingArrangements profile. His goal was to build a 420-friendly, culturally vegan mansion in the middle of the city full of, I assume, stinky hippie chicks. He had grown up with money, played professional baseball in an obscure European country like Sweden or Norway or something. Then he pivoted to professional gambling—poker, I think. Then, seeking fame along with his fortune, he started a YouTube channel back in the website's heyday. He focused on videos about *wild* and *epic* facts about nature, talked about owls and snakes while standing in front of a green screen with his 6'5" charisma and a cheap safari cap. He amassed a couple hundred thousand subscribers. I started working for him a couple of years after his internet fame, when he decided to pivot from on-screen talent into the business of underpaying listless art school dropouts to crank out content for him instead. All of us in the content factory were paid $16.20 an hour and he'd get $10,000 per video or more. We produced two to five videos a day, five days a week.

After a year and a half, I'd saved enough money for a vacation. I was friends with the office manager and also very depressed, palpably so. A reprieve from this life was definitely in order. I was 20 years old and all my friends had moved out of Vegas to pursue an education, many of them in the arts. I stayed behind with my shitty dad in this shitty city to make fake art at my shitty fake job. But it's not like I had a college tuition or student loans to worry about–plus, officially I did not have to pay my dad rent. While he liked to occasionally invent some sort of impending financial destitution to guilt me into coughing up a couple hundred dollars, through some mathematical eventuation, he'd left me alone for the last couple of months—long enough for me to save up for this vacation. My dad warned me about drugs, how they fuck you up, and I promised him that my friends and I would behave while I was away. I just needed some time off.

* * *

Seattle called out to me primarily because several of my internet friends that I'd known since I was twelve lived there. I've always struggled to find a word that appropriately describes my relationship to them. *Chosen family* sounds so sad and cliché and besides, our connections feel much more *fated* than chosen. The most accurate title exists somewhere between "universally predestined family" and "my childhood friends."

Seattle was a city by the ocean, it had semi-functioning public transit and lush greenery. It had vegan restaurants aplenty and artists walking around looking all obviously artist-y—lugging around their supplies, wearing weird outfits like three-piece suits scavenged from a thrift store, and looking generally pissed off at society. Everything that I couldn't easily find in my life in the desert.

One of the first nights I was there, I'd slept over at a friend's apartment, an upperclassman from my high school named Leila. She'd graduated a year before me and had made a life for herself out in Washington studying botany and making coffee for money. Her entire apartment was covered in anatomical drawings of mushrooms and plants, a Riso print of a topographical depiction of soil on one wall. I was in awe of how much space she had to herself and how much independence she seemed to have. Living alone, being surrounded by beautiful art, not dealing with some shitty boss or shitty dad. This world seemed surreal and heavenly.

I'm not exactly sure why or how, but her eight inch by twelve inch by six inch freezer was filled to the brim with marijuana brownies. I think her friend, a dealer, wanted to store them at her house out of paranoia that he'd get busted with them—or maybe it was because he didn't own a freezer himself? In exchange for her storage service, Leila could have as many brownies as she wanted. She admitted to me that she was too scared to try them on her own. She, now emboldened by my presence, and I, emboldened by my complete ignorance about the quantities of marijuana contained within one brownie, reached in and grabbed some. We each unwrapped our own brownies and ate them entirely.

My subsequent trip coincided with a show in which Nicole Dollanganger and Wavves were performing—two extremely Tumblr musical acts that were all the rage within my circles at the time. A couple of hours after swallowing five times the recommended dosage of cannabis, Leila and I ventured into Lower Queen Anne, walking underneath the Space Needle. I stared up at the giant tower. It looked exactly how it looked in pictures. Maybe smaller than the Stratosphere, Las Vegas's blatant impersonation. But still. Tall. Darkness fell onto the city and my pot-addled vision began to tighten, my peripheries going dark. I was walking into a new dimension, parallel to Seattle but more topsy-turvy.

Nicole Dollanganger sang a lot of sad girl love songs with her falsetto voice, the perfect kind of airy music that sad teenagers listen to in their dark bedrooms after school. But for this tour, she was traveling with a heavy metal band. I'd thought the brownie had already taken its effect on me, but an entirely new tidal wave of cannabinoids crashed into my bloodstream in the middle of her set, forcing my body into a right angle so that I was cracked at the hip. I leaned onto Leila—a very tiny white girl who stood at about chest-high to me—so that I wouldn't fall over. As Nicole hymned about horny teenage melancholy, her band shredded, tearing the air with heavy sonic blasts of bass and drums. Nicole's quiet, siren-like singing cutting through the heavy velvet thrum of her band sent me into a trance. The crowd started to separate and a dark portal spread out like a bloodstain on the floor. I watched demons and gargoyles fly out from hell and swirl around the crowd, filling the open air above us with their sick vibes. They weren't evil, they were just, like, adding to the ambiance. After her set, I went outside by the fountain and rocked back and forth in the fetal position, pushing away the green fractals at the edge of my vision. It took several years for me to realize that the visit from the underworld was all a hallucination. So much of it was so new to me: Seattle, the sound of Nicole's voice against the steely bass, being away from my family, the edibles. I'd assumed the demons from hell were simply a part of the show. Maybe this is how people got down outside of Nevada. The next morning I had breakfast and lunch with my universally-predestined family by the Puget Sound, zenning out amongst all the wet blue air and alcoholic kombucha. Then, I got on a train to Portland to spend some time with Solito, my genderqueer soulmate. Solito and I got along well because we both had to grow up too quickly—our parents forced us to pay bills, work, all while maintaining our heavy courseload. We both felt older than our classmates, and we were both proto-nonbinary, hated being referred to as a boy or as a girl and lumping ourselves together whenever we could to avoid being gendered in class. We both bleached our dark curly hair into technicolor streaks, shaved our heads into extreme undercuts, wore cut-off overalls and platform shoes, both knew exactly how to take life unseriously because everything in our life was always so serious. When Sol accepted a scholarship to attend art school in Portland, I felt both relief and preemptive grief. I was glad that they'd get away from their parents, finally have some agency over their life—but I knew that someone who really understood me would be really far away. I was excited to see them again.

* * *

Bong rip. Vegan omelet. Music videos—FKA Twigs, M.I.A., Lady Gaga. Joint lit. Chilaquiles, walk to the park. More bong rips. House party, house show, Pabst Blue Ribbon, pissing in an alley, passing a joint, more music videos. Morning again.

I'd smoked weed back in Vegas, but never like this. All of my stoner friends up North had such high tolerances that they'd chain smoke weed like Marlboros and I simply joined them, assuming it was a normal quantity to consume. Even if it wasn't—this was my vacation, right? Even compared to my other Northerner Stoner Friends, Solito could really handle their greens in a way that I could only attempt, but I wanted to do as the real adults who left our hometown do, so I did my best anyway, spending multiple nights in a row greening out. A couple of bleary days passed like this, punctuated with the spark of lighters and the occasional meal from a vegan diner—and then, it was time to meet the Prince.

We'd agreed to meet at an arcade with a bar, which felt distinct from the barcades in Las Vegas. Those are more like a bar with a wimpy selection of games and a basketball simulator, a Chuck E. Cheese for adults. Which is to say, lame. This place was not lame. It was full of technicolor vintage arcade boxes, nerdy games that nerds journey across state lines to play. On the second floor we played a round of Dance Dance Revolution and both self-consciously decide to stop when we realize we were starting to get sweaty and musky, a stinky wet fog threatening to break out from our creases.

We'd run out of quarters rather quickly and decided to go for a walk to the waterfront —she knew the way. The Prince seemed to know everything about the city: its history, its secret spots. I did not smoke any weed that morning, so I could see clearly now, although I had no idea what parts of the city I'd spent time in over the last couple of days (which only seemed to highlight the magical quality of her knowledge). She told me she liked to take long walks to get away from her life, and those long walks lent themselves to getting to know her city very intimately. We found her favorite bench in front of one of the rivers—maybe not her favorite-favorite but definitely a good one. I could tell she'd spent a couple of hours sitting there before.

We opened our sketchbooks and traded them. We were both artists—I suppose we both still are artists, but we were young and earnest artists then. The kind of artists who carried around art supplies to dates and exchanged sketchbooks to leave each other drawings but had no aspirations or concrete plans to make a living off of their work.

I sketched a cartoon portrait of what I saw. Sleepy eyes, killer calves, a strong and very cute nose. When we trade them back, we effuse each other with compliments and smiles.

The sun was setting, but I didn't want to stop hanging out. I don't remember our conversation at all, but I remember that it felt like entering a private little world. A world where all the details seemed familiar and brand new at the same time.

I invited her to come hang out at Solito's house. We could watch music videos and get high and all be together in a big friendship bubble. Just friendship—nothing else, obviously.

In Solito's living room, a bong appeared by itself and we all took bubbly rips, watched more FKA Twigs music videos *(You haven't seen the music video for "Glass & Patron"?!)* until the sun really did set, and it became dark and then darker and then threatened to become light again soon.

Solito and their roommate retreated to their rooms for the night, perhaps sensing a vibe that the the Prince and I were too oblivious to see. I asked the Prince how far away she lived, if she needed to go, and she lingered in the room with me. The trains weren't going to start running again for a few hours anyway.

I wanted to touch her, hold her hand. Maybe look deeply into her eyes and see if I could see in her mind what I felt in mine. A deep, perturbing movement at my core. The chemical attraction that the body understands and the mind doesn't. Instead, we both fell asleep adjacent to each other on Solito's giant bean bag.

When the sun came up, I walked her to the train and we said goodbye with a hug. The Prince smelled like eucalyptus and tea tree oil and something sharp and sparkly, unplaceable, her unique human musk. I walked back to Solito's in the soft powder blue of morning, grateful for this little adventure away from the desert.

Later, I'd learn that the Prince wanted to kiss me too.

* * *

This is what my first boyfriend was like: I was in 3rd grade. His name was Daniel and he was Filipino and Chinese. He had eyes that seemed to be permanently smiling. We had a uniform in elementary school, but he always wore a long sleeve shirt under his little Polo. Usually, just a black or white waffle knit. But sometimes he wore a long sleeve with flames climbing up the arms. He always came in first during foot races.

This is what my first girlfriend was like: I was in 3rd grade. Her name was Lynn and she was Mexican and Chinese. She had long black hair that I admired and envied in equal parts. She always wore her uniform with the school-issued crewneck, the sleeves stretched out over her fingers. Her handwriting was neat and bubbly.

At some point during my 3rd grade career, I had convinced Lynn and Daniel, separately, to be my special friends. I distinctly remember that I did not call them my girlfriend and boyfriend, and those labels are probably not accurate to what 3rd graders are doing on the playground. But I felt sparkly feelings in my heart when I talked to these special friends. At some point, I made them hold each of my hands as we walked up the hill to the playground for recess, and we marched along in a little daisy chain of polyamorous elementary school children.

Then and now, the prevalent script for heteronormative love—in which one's life is centered upon finding a lifelong partner and then the gravity shifts and that one person becomes the main and only person in your life— baffled me. I did not, do not, want to choose among all the loves of my life, my friends, my family, my interests, myself.

That sort of relationship is not what I saw growing up. I was raised by my parents, my grandma, my aunts, my parents' friends, my ninongs and ninangs. I was surrounded by my sister, my cousins, play cousins, neighbors. I spent equal time with all these people in my village. And my parents spent as much time with other people—or alone—as they did with each other. Ultimately, they separated and got divorced, but what I'm saying is, I never saw that classic romantic relationship, marriage-centric lifestyle modeled for me. My aunts and uncles were mostly single or had spouses working back in the Philippines. Everyone did it differently, but no one did it in the nuclear style that they like to have on old TV shows.

When I met my universally predestined family at twelve years old, they anchored the center of my life like a network of fungi. Despite meeting on the internet and being separated by hundreds of miles, we found ways to constantly communicate and support each other. We'd talk online, via instant messengers and video calls and phone calls, we'd send each other money for meals and advise each other through life's hurdles. We'd visit when we were traveling, host each other, feed each other in real life when it was possible. For so long, it felt like they were doing most of the work raising me.

When I got to high school, I found a real life network of support in my friends. All of us weirdos among weirdos gravitating towards each other despite everything: different zip codes, different class schedules, different academic foci. We laughed together, looked at the world together, cut school together, smoked weed for the first time together, cheated off of each other's homework, shared meals paid for by our combined meager budgets. This network was added to my network of internet friends. It was a love that was so expansive and so affectionate and caring, I could not imagine that a singular person would give me what all of this friendship gave me.

* * *

In high school I'd had a few half-hearted attempts at that classic movie romance, the kind where you like someone and go on a date with them and try to make out or something. A couple of artsy boys took an interest in me, finding me during class or between periods to ask me about my opinions on jazz or Camus or the Baroque period or whatever gossip was circulating around the student body at the time. At the time, they annoyed me. Our school was one of those magnet schools for art and the student demographics skewed distinctly female—something like eight girls for every two boys. Any dude who didn't smell like sewage or did not seem obviously 100% homosexual instantly jumped to the top of the food chain. Because the boys talking to me weren't the faggy kinds nor the sewage types, I assumed they were straight dudes being pests, trying to set me up for some sort of humiliation or otherwise waste my time with their male shenanigans.

But, eventually I got the hint that some of their interest was genuine—it wasn't the windup to a hate crime, it was teenage curiosity.

Sometimes, I did indulge the artsy boys in their interests, but they all ended so tragically. Once I'd gone on a painfully platonic walk with this dude who played jazz. We walked around Fashion Show mall, a place on The Strip that catered primarily to tourists. Named after its gimmick: a runway would rise up from the ground in the middle of the mall for fashion shows—seriously, models, local designers, a DJ pumping questionable beats. Don't get me wrong, I love doing touristy shit in Vegas, walking around a mall anywhere in America is interesting with the right person. The runway did not come up from the ground during this date though, and the conversation didn't go anywhere fun either.

Once, an upperclassman who fancied himself a poet, asked me out on a date to get some Thai food. He was cute, a chubby ginger guy with blue-green eyes. The date was horrible, though. After the pad see ew and curry arrived, he brought the noodles close to him and told me he wasn't really interested in sharing the dishes, even though we had run through the menu and decided on optimal dishes to order together. Who the hell gets Thai food and doesn't eat family style? Then he showed me his poetry zine that he happened to bring and read them to me. I'm totally a sucker for poets, but his stuff was seriously bad. The kind of poetry white people write that has no emotional honesty and is all about experimenting with form. Like, cool, a whole page that's just one word repeated over and over again. Is this supposed to be sexy? He left the check on the table for a good forty-five minutes and then performatively checked his phone when I finally opened it and read the price aloud.

On the drive back to his house, my bank account approximately two Thai dinners lighter, I got a call from my mom who informed me that my uncle had just died. I turned to chubby ginger poet and said, "You know, I'd love to ask you to make out at this point, but my uncle just died so I have to go home." I kicked him out of my Prius, laughing in shock and because it was all, objectively, hilarious.

At some point during my sophomore year, I got sucked into the orbit of a popular girl in the visual arts department, which I was also studying. Zoey had a penchant for painting noses and social manipulation. She was a junior, but we had mutual internet friends who connected me to her and her friend group. It was a confusing friendship, primarily because I hadn't had many friends in real life before, and my newfound high school friends my age were still fresh. Zoey would do this thing where she'd declare some opinion she had about a new trend, a book everyone was reading or a TV show everyone was obsessed with, and bring judgment upon anyone—including her friends— who disagreed with her. When one of us would echo that same opinion a couple of days later, she'd scoff and wonder why we cared so much about a TV show or say that she'd started watching it and that she actually liked it very much. We never knew where we stood with Zoey.

It was also confusing because, at the time, I thought I was this very obviously faggy gay boy. Despite that, I'd fallen into what I now recognize as an intense psychosexual sapphic dynamic with Zoey. She recognized the girl in me, I saw the dyke in her, and we gravitated towards each other. I was obsessed with making sure Zoey thought highly of me, with spending time with her. I received her words like they were gospel. Once during a group hangout at someone's house we sat in a big cushiony loveseat and idly cuddled while we watched the TV show she once declared she hated.

That's all to say, I didn't really understand what was going on, but after a year of Zoey I knew I did not like how she made me feel. After a few confusing sob sessions in the shower, I broke up with her (even though we weren't dating). I don't remember exactly how I did it, being emotionally shattered by this weird non-relationship and teenage hormones and everything, but it was probably over text. I think her next boyfriend after me was a suspiciously femme gay boy too.

After all this romantic failure, I delved deep into the whole faggy nympho thing. No more feelings, no more boys my age. Instead: Craigslist, Grindr, cruising in public. I'd found lots of sexual gratification with strange men of all kinds, anonymously pounding and slurping away. Dicks huge and small stretching open my jaw with slobber. Dudes pushing me over onto the bed to slam into me. There were a lot of bodies crashing into each other, but not a lot of meeting of the minds. When it came to soft feelings, emotions, and warmth, I could just turn to my friends instead.

It wasn't until that autumn, years later as an adult, when I met the Prince, where things finally felt different. When I found something soft and special, something erotic and sentimental. We were drawn to each other intellectually and chemically.

I had a crush.

* * *

The next couple of months after that long date with the Prince were full of texting and co-watching movies over Skype or starting a movie at the same time on Netflix while we sat on the phone together. She sent me a video of herself playing guitar and singing with a fake credit roll at the end that shouted me out in particular, although I didn't really do much to warrant a credit. We'd text each other all day, me at my office job committing time theft on my phone and her, dictating replies into her Apple Watch while she stocked shelves at the co-op.

Hilariously, it would take a couple of months of this gross lover-birdy behavior for us to realize that our feelings for each other had moved beyond platonic friendship.

Sex with the Prince was carnal and explosive and hungry. After we'd confessed our feelings for each other over the phone, the floodgates opened. She'd stacked a couple of her vacation days together to create a long weekend from work and visit me in Vegas. I picked her up from the airport and we did not make it out of Arrivals. We slid into the back of my Prius and made out, a wet storm of kisses with a lot of grabbing. Our pants unbuckled and slid under our butts, we shifted our bodies to fit perfectly in the cramped backseat of my hatchback. We clawed out a rubber from the stack buried in the console for all my faggy nympho shenanigans and fucked. We were puzzle pieces, suited to fit together, our torsos and legs and cock and vagina sliding perfectly into place. I'd fucked before, gotten feral, but never felt this comfortable while doing so, never felt like I belonged beside someone like this. We clawed at each other in a way that I'd never experienced before with the strange men I crawled into beds and trucks and bathroom stalls with. There was a mutual desire that was so all-encompassing that whenever we could get naked, we flew into each other like magnets. We had sex like we were trying to fuse our molecules together to create one singular new being. When it was time to finally stop obviously fucking in the Arrivals garage, I cracked our windows so that the hot, steamy sweat from our bodies could pour out of the car and rejoin the atmosphere.

* * *

When her lease was up at her apartment in Portland, I told her about my idea. She should move to Las Vegas! In with me! The idea, rightfully, scared her. I was a couple of years younger and a virtual stranger. Yes, she'd visited Vegas once over the last couple of months and we'd spent plenty of hours together over the phone, but we'd had so little actual time in real life together. I'm really good at convincing people to give me what I want, though, especially if I believe it's a good idea.

I flew over to her apartment back in the PNW a couple of weeks later and helped her pack her stuff into the back of a truck. We drove off back to the desert to start our new life together. I drove the U-Haul for seventeen hours straight, taking a brief two hour nap in the parking lot of a McDonald's in Reno.

* * *

Our life together was beautiful and hard. Two queer kids trying to make a life without help from our families, not a college degree between us—barely two high school degrees at that. We managed to carve a life out for ourselves in the slums of Las Vegas. It went like this:

First, a stint at my horrible dad's house full of tense conversations and cultural misunderstandings. Plus, a lot of grandstanding by my narcissistic father. Once, he drunkenly, "playfully," slapped the Prince in the middle of a Bacchanalian baby shower for my half-sister.

From there, a month at my best friend Mollie's mother's house. Mollie and the Prince got along swimmingly during her pre-U-Haul visit, and when queers can't afford to live on their own, we flock together. At Mollie's house, we whiled away dark summer nights in the suburbs—a different one than my dad's, but still the suburbs. Mostly we played poker in the hot spare bedroom that Mollie's late grandmother used to live in, using quarters and dimes as chips. After a few weeks of that, weeks of the Prince and I both misunderstanding the idiosyncrasies of Mollie's mother and hiding from her mild disdain in the bedroom—the three of us had saved up enough money to make it on our own.

We found a cave-like apartment behind a Best Buy near the university. To my young, plebian eyes, it was cute. The apartment was a part of a larger complex, each building a quadplex, ours was 1B. We kept ourselves safe with what felt like queer magic—1A, 2A, and 2B all got broken into and robbed, but I never felt like I was in danger there. I felt like we were home. Sure, the alley between us and the Best Buy housed a dumpster which liked to regularly catch on blue electrical fire, but we lived walking distance to two Asian grocery stores. Score!

* * *

Sex between the Prince and I did not stay all-encompassing and feral. Even though we'd succeeded in scrounging together a life, it was hard. We all worked ourselves to the bone so that we could have enough to cover our bills and enough—just barely, but enough—to eat.

I wasn't fully cognizant of another element, but I see now in hindsight that it was hard to deal with the monogamy, the nuclear family structure we organized our life into. I'd missed the freedom of slutting around and being a fag. What the Prince and I had felt like forever. It was this solid thing, not like some of the other relationships I'd seen my peers get into—obviously toxic dynamics that should end sooner rather than later. The Prince and I saw eye to eye. We loved each other. That scared me. I looked into the future and I saw us together, decade in, decade out. It didn't feel like I made a mistake bringing the Prince all the way to Vegas, which scared me even more. I felt like this version of my youth was meant to be full of bad dates and trial boyfriends. Instead, the potential for all of these sexy shenanigans was dissolving in my hands. We always had polyamorous, non monogamous inclinations, but they were more in theory than in practice. There weren't a lot of eligible singles to play with in Vegas. Plus, we were so busy surviving, stealing, working, and spending time with each other, we didn't really make time to look for anyone else to mess around with. So, even though we were this queer family, making a theoretically non monogamous queer life together, a lot of what we were doing matched up with nuclear family dynamics. Breadwinner, homemaker, lots of bills to pay, lots of chores to do, commuting. A lot of that magic we felt early on had snuck out the window when we weren't looking.

* * *

We shared so much together, clinging onto each other out of love, yes, and also out of necessity. We knew we could not survive without the other, emotionally and materially. Frequently, we'd only ever have one job between us, forcing us to steal, hustle, beg, and scrape together what we had to make our life. I'd felt like it was mostly on me to do the larger share of the stealing, hustling, and begging. Whereas my survival tactic was desperate struggling, flailing against the clutches of predatory capitalism with all my might, it felt like the Prince was meditating. Waiting out the drought, like a cactus in the steppe. Less movement, slowing down, waiting for something to happen. I don't think this is necessarily true. Most of us in the margins of the machine, under the heel of the boot, do whatever we can to make it out alive. But there, in the thick of it, I felt like my ally, my accomplice, was not always there for me the way I wanted her to be. I didn't want to survive and merely make it out of each month alive. I wanted to kick the world's ass and take what I felt was rightfully mine.

Capitalism had poisoned the reservoir of our love and tainted my heart with resentment. The kind of resentment that rots—slowly, but still, rots.

After the pandemic had turned the Prince's brief hiatus from work into several long years of unemployment, I took it upon myself to don the title of breadwinner, matriarch—I became our queer family's assigned worrier.

My job had converted into a remote position in the pandemic, so at least I could keep my income—only my job got much harder without extra pay. But even before that, I'd do whatever I could to meet the gap between what our income was and what our bills asked us to cough up. I could write, so I could pick up a little side hustle and sell some SEO-friendly articles here and there to grab us extra coin.

Back in my nympho fag days, I'd done some more harrowing jobs, meeting up with johns I'd gotten off of Craigslist, worried that they were a cop trying to catch me in the act. Luckily most of the jobs I took around this time were relatively chill. One man, allegedly a CEO of a medical tech company, wanted to blow off some steam away from his stressful life and boring wife to spend time with trans women. We met in the food court inside of a casino in Vegas's old downtown—a strange combination of chain fast food and bespoke mom and pop restaurants. We walked around, casino to casino, and he showed me how to gamble. I've got dyscalculia so numbers get all scrambled in my head and stress me out. CEO was a genius with numbers, though. At a craps machine he told me the odds of each bet and showed me how to easily build up a jackpot. He instructed me to bet on twelve and told me which buttons to press. Magically, I won. The machine coughs up $120, which he handed to me nonchalantly.

Once, a bald vegetarian wanted me to spend time with him while he was in town for work. We walked around the mall and he bought me a new pair of panties so he could see me put them on in the dark alley we parked in. He gave me a couple of twenties and included the cheap panties as a part of my payment.

In the end, I was too befuddled by the stress of being an inexperienced sex worker, of talking to a new client and trying to be sexy, and by all the numbers he rattled off at me, to make for good conversation, so he ultimately waved goodbye. Other jobs were less peaceful—during one job, a downtrodden dad asked to eat my ass—which he did, exclusively, for hours. I ask if he wants, like, a blowjob or something, to which he asks if he can just keep licking my ass. I mean, yeah. When Downtrodden Dad is done, I walk out of the living room and see that his kids are home, watching TV loudly in the living room. I'm standing there in a cartoonishly slutty outfit, the kind of short skirt, fishnets, slutty camisole that hookers on TV wear when they're getting arrested. He offers to drive me back to my neighborhood and I, not wanting to lose any of my profit on an Uber, say yes. My skin goes ice cold when he shepherds in his kids into the car behind me, because it's time to take them to their mom's. I wonder if they'll tell their mom about their dad's weird new friend.

Now, my hustle had moved on from un-fun, low-paying sex work jobs into freelance writing and radio work, doing remote labor from my computer in our bedroom, plugging into the screen so I could make ends meet. But I felt resentful, not necessarily towards the Prince, but in general. Why was I forced to entertain weird men for chump change, commit petty theft, and make art for millionaires so I could dig myself out of the hole I was born into?

I did my best to hold all of my angst privately, not wanting to burden my beloved family with the stress of making sure our apartment stayed our apartment and our bellies stayed fed, not wanting to burden them with the unchangeable fact of our caste. But it poured out, into cold shoulders and irritability, into tense sentences and bitterness. I often felt like it was me scouting alone into the dark and trying to make sure everyone else was okay. Typical Virgo shit.

I tried to place the blame on capitalism, on the American government, hurling curses at whatever was left of Ronald Reagan's decayed remains for making our life so fucking hard, hoping he was being tortured somewhere in the afterlife. I'd look up at the dark ceiling at night and take deep breaths, send my anger toward this modern world and how it failed us. Then I'd roll over and spoon my Prince.

But even those little prayers against capitalism didn't stop the death of our sex life. I'd felt like I'd given so much of myself to the Prince, to our family, in every axis of our life, that I instinctively closed myself off in the bedroom. I felt like I had given everything of myself to everyone else. Everything we had, we shared, and everything we had came from my hard work, sweat, and blood. I could not bear to be the mother and the fucker.

* * *

After seven years together, I took a long trip to L.A. for work. This was the last nail in the coffin. That week away was happy and peaceful. The Prince and I did not miss each other. Now that we lived in Chicago, our life expanded outwards and did not need to revolve around each other in our pandemic apartment. The Prince had her own friends, a job in nightlife. We rarely saw each other that much now anyway. She'd be gone when I woke up, and I'd be asleep when she came back. This trip away felt a lot like a simulation of what our lives could be if we were single. I'd no longer go to bed expecting someone to be sleeping beside me, she'd no longer come home to a bed with a sleeping girlfriend filling our bedroom with bitter psychic energy. As soon as I returned, the two of us talked in our bedroom about how happy we were the last week apart. Hammer. Nail. Coffin. Grave.

* * *

This was a love that transformed me. The Prince shepherded me into so many new versions of myself—a 20-year-old fag trying to make it on his own for the first time, a newly-out trans girl taking her glamour out for a spin, a nonmonogamous lifestyle. Together we put on many masks: husband, wife, lover, kids-raising-each-other, die hard friends. Together we were gay boys, dykes, trans4trans, we were roommates and then, briefly, bitter exes forced to live together. We put on masks that were uncomfortable and wore them for so long we forgot what it was like to breathe, unfettered. I pushed myself to the absolute ends of the earth for the Prince and I saw how far I could go—and saw how far was too far.

I'd willingly put on this mask for the Prince—a mask that the Prince did not ask me to wear—and then I subsequently felt trapped in it. I'd become someone I did not like, I became resentful and cold and stingy with my affection. My love was not given freely in hugs, kisses, fucks, and attention—I doled it out to her to keep our life together afloat. This life that neither of us seemed particularly happy to be living.

* * *

On the first day alone in my new single person apartment, I found an old photograph of the Prince and me in an old box of knick knacks. The two of us smiling and kissing, a grinning selfie in which our cheeks are touching in the back of an open U-Haul, all of her things stacked to the brim. A picture of her lounging in bed, light shining on her face, just so. I remembered how much I loved her at the beginning of everything, how my love burned passionate and bright and unapologetic. In those pictures, I saw how much I'd changed over the years. How my love became cold and obligatory. How I didn't show her off like I used to. How I'd become ashamed of who I was and who she was.

When we broke up, she stopped being my Prince. She needed to become someone new. And so did I. I'm so glad we set ourselves free and broke up, that she pushed me to move out and figure out a new version of our lives. I'm in it now, in that big open freedom of fresh heartbreak. Not beholden to any roles or definitions I confined myself to for the sake of nobody. I feel a deep and profound freedom—the same freedom I felt when I first transitioned. Euphoric. Terrifying. Boundless.

SEXTING IS ROLEPLAY ABOUT DESIRE

I want to sit in your truck and talk about nothing

I want to put up Christmas lights with you in our townhouse and walk through the snow

I want to hug you for a while under layers and layers of blankets in our California King

I want to bite your neck and drain your blood like a vampire

I want to be a machine that smells your armpits and measures how much to pay for your labor

I want to kiss you in a shower with a window that has the blurry thing on it

I want to sit on a blanket in a quiet forest and wrap my legs around you

I want to read erotic literature to you on a shag rug surrounded by pillows

I want to build a chair and sit on it while you sit on my lap

I want to get promoted at work and hire you as my assistant and start an illicit affair

I want to live in your walls and listen to your footsteps as you walk around

I want to go on a date with you at a restaurant and be told that you already secretly paid for it

I want to sit around a giant pot of hot soup and eat it with you forever and I want to never get full

I want to sign a lease with you and break it and sign another lease with you

I want to ride an eight hour plane across the ocean with you and pat your back while you puke

I want to marry you and get divorced and reconnect with you 20 years later when we're old

I want to move to a villa in Tuscany and meet you for the first time in my garden

I want to transform into a beetle and live in a tiny plastic box in your house

I want to watch you die young and then die in my old age and fuck you in heaven

GOING HOME (OR BEDROOM ENVY)

For a couple of years, Emma and I had slowly faded from being best friends to people who went to high school together. Everything is so hard in your early 20s—at least for us it was. Trying to keep our mind, spirit, and body all stitched together without the structure provided by the pursuit of an undergraduate degree, trying to pay our bills and make it on our own, trying to heal from the last two decades of being raised by our psycho parents. Now that we weren't compelled to see each other every day at school, maintaining our friendship slowly and surely fell in priority. But, after some distance from a toxic mutual friends, during a period in the pandemic when it felt safe to gather again, we reunited over dinner. I was glad that we were becoming close again, and I remembered how much I loved her as we ate piles of sashimi in the middle of the desert. Then, in the middle of our second course, she confessed that she was moving to Chicago to be closer to her new (currently long-distance) boyfriend, Tyler, and our other best friend Allessandra. Without thinking, I said, "I'll come too!"

I had been plotting to get my queer family out of the city, I just didn't know where. I knew we should move north, out from the drier and drier drought-ridden desert that was getting hotter every year. I'm not very good at arithmetic but I did the math: Lake Mead was running out of water, the planet was getting hotter, and the people in charge were building more casinos for more of the Californian transplants. It was time to go. When Emma pointed me to Chicago, it all aligned: the Midwest would be more tolerable in the turbulence of climate catastrophe. There would be a huge source of fresh water (ideal for the water wars everyone keeps forebodingly predicting)a semi-reliable public transit system for our car-less hippie lifestyle. I used to be afraid to leave the West Coast and its eternal temperance, afraid of a winter that snows. But the same way climate change was making our summers longer and hotter, it was making the north's winters shorter and warmer and therefore more hospitable to a desert lizard like me. Okay, I thought. We could live there.

Because we didn't have the resources to fly to Chicago early and go apartment hunting, we relied on some queer broker I found online to do some apartment hunting and to set us up with a place. Eventually, he found us a spot in Logan Square in a building he knew we'd get into if we fudged certain parts of our application, left the part out where we have two cats and where two out of four potential tenants didn't have jobs lined up.

Emma, the Prince, my trans sister Audrey, and I all moved into this slum sight unseen. At first, the building was exciting—all of Chicago is. We're moved in May, in Chicago's wet spring, on the precipice of warmer weather, and the city is *huge,* its skyscrapers taller than the ones in Vegas, and so many of the buildings are older than the oldest buildings I grew up around. The city teems with potential energy, and its thrum distracted us from the early warning signs that this first apartment would be less than ideal. Emma and I arrived first in her 2003 Nissan packed to the brim with houseplants and loose luggage that couldn't fit into our shared moving pod. We found what the apartment held for us: one very large centipede, very little closet space, and one naughty poltergeist that liked to leave mysterious puddles of blood around the apartment, walk around with heavy, wet footsteps, and unintelligibly whisper in your ear if you went to the kitchen alone at night.

We spent most of the first few months getting to know our new home *outside* our home. I spent most of my time catching up with other friends who lived in the city, getting to know the neighborhoods, taking public transit up and down and all around (getting on a train felt to go somewhere felt so novel!), eating up all the food, laying in all the parks, going on dates, staring at the lake. When I was home, I was working one of the three remote jobs I had and was absorbed so deeply in my computer I didn't really notice the pests or the creaky floorboards or the poltergeist haunting my roomies.

Winter eventually arrived to put a stop to our adventures—sure, a mild winter, apparently due to global warming, but more than mildly perturbing nonetheless. Even though BP and Shell and Lockheed Martin had all taken the bite out of a midwestern winter, the prospect of spending more than a twenty-four hours in temperatures below forty-five degrees scared all of us shitless. Winter in Las Vegas does exist, but it's a windy and dark cold, a season that does not frequently dip into freezing temperatures, let alone snow. This winter everyone kept saying was so mild still brought with it a polar vortex, a cold snap that briefly brought the "feels like" temperature down to negative fifty degrees Fahrenheit—literally colder than the South Pole at the time. Of course, I took advantage of my suffering and posted a screenshot of my weather app to make sure everyone viewing my Instagram stories back home felt sorry for me. It got so cold that it hurts to go outside without a million layers of thermals and furs on, and the giant shearling jacket I ordered was so heavy it made my shoulders sore—for the most part, I stayed home.

The poltergeist that I thought was a quirky and mostly funny trait of living in a pre-war building seemed to be haunting everyone else worse than me. Everyone kept telling me about nightmares haunted by a shadowy man and forcing themselves to ignore the presence in the kitchen at night to get water. I did feel a smidge jealous that the ghost did not whisper unintelligible things into *my* ears at night, but when everyone else in the apartment told me that it happened to them semi-regularly, I realized we'd have to do some negotiating with the spirit. When we first moved in we attempted a classic, basic witchy move of cleansing the space with smoke and salt and mopping the floor—but with all the haunting going on, perhaps all we did was make the ghost living in the apartment angry. After all, it was there first! So, I concocted a plan to make an offering of peace—to tell the ghost *Thanks for having us, let's coexist here together.* I produced a hitherto unused thrift shop glass candy bowl I thought I would fill with my estrogen pills *á* la *Valley of the Dolls* and instead filled it with rice and dried lavender. Emma, Audrey, and the Prince, who all worked at the same bar, had cash tips and quarters for our coin-op laundry machine, so we fold the money into neat origami flowers and fans and stuck it into the bowl. I remember reading that when offering food to ancestors, they like things that smell strong and taste sweet, so Audrey stuck some loose candies from Chinatown into the bowl and I spiked in a couple of DumDums I bought to sate an oral fixation and wear as an accessory. Finally, we all offered some incense and arranged it into the bowl so it looked sort of like a radial sun and a crown at the same time, but decided to keep them unlit since the initial cleansing smoke thing seemed only to make the apartment spirit angry with us. I placed the bowl on our mantle in the living room and the four of us thought grateful thoughts for the ghost.

* * *

Our slumlord property managers had neglected to maintain the building's boilers—despite our weeks of complaining about funky radiators—leaving forty-eight units without heat. When we fought back, organized, and got half the building to withhold rent in protest, they responded in-kind months later when many of our leases were up for renewal. Thirty percent rent hikes in already overpriced apartments, no negotiations considered. So, even though the ghost had now resigned to a non-menacing coexistence with us, we'd still have to make our trek out from Logan Square to wherever else the city would take us.

Emma would move in with Tyler into their own spot, which left me, the Prince, and Audrey to find ours. Audrey and the Prince worked full time at the bar—a physically and mentally grueling job that took up many hours of their night and led them to spend many hours of the day sleeping and resting. Because I was the privileged girl who worked flexible hours from her computer wherever the hell she wanted, I made it my duty to do all the admin work of apartment hunting for us. I quickly learned that being in the city only made apartment hunting marginally easier. Now, instead of getting on FaceTime with a broker who drove out to apartments in my stead, I'd have to physically go to places myself and coordinate with a whole slew of agents and brokers. I ended up working with a very hyper Mexican man in his early forties who talked fast and braggadociously about his lifestyle, his baby, his body, his sexy Filipino wife, his famous Filipino stepson who had been cast in a recent blockbuster horror movie, and his famous Filipino stepson's body. To prove his adjacency to fame, he video called Famous Filipino Stepson in the car while we traveled from one apartment showing to the next, but Hollywood Actor Son had to hang up on us rather quickly because he was currently on set filming his *next* blockbuster movie. I realized later he was either on some yet-to-be-regulated pre-workout supplement or snorting some sort of upper when I wasn't looking. Eventually, Hyper Man gives up on me when he realizes my credit is below 700 and I won't be bagging him an easy commission. Apartment hunting becomes my part-time job between all my other part-time jobs, like it's my hobby to open all of the listings on all of the sites, to send messages out about seeing apartments, some of them I don't really like as I get more and more desperate and more and more tired. I start to wonder if we'll ever find somewhere else to live. I can't let it happen, of course, we won't be homeless. But the path between where we are now and our new home gets foggier by the day.

As I'm running around the city trudging through the musty, mostly dilapidated apartments that we might be able to afford, a bunch of people were scheduling visits to our previously-haunted slummy apartment. Many of them are a bunch of random queers coming through our apartment, and I see in them what me and my family looked like when we first moved in. They look past all of our junky alleyway furniture and see potential for new lives, their eyes dreamy and bright. I want to warn them about the slumlords, about the lack of heat. I want to crush their dreams and tell them to look somewhere else, that this apartment has the illusion of being big, but really it's cramped, and the hallways are long and creaky. Most of them ignore us, or look at us like it's our fault the apartment is shitty, and maybe it is, but I swear it's not us, it's the ghost, the unfriendly layout of the building that turns it into an alley with bedrooms, and a kitchen tucked around the back in the haunted zone. It's the slumlords breaking our spirits with no heat, gaslighting all of us into thinking we don't deserve to live in a comfortable little hole despite paying nearly $2,000 a month for it. We'd have our shit together if it weren't for that, we'd have a home.

But I give the same hopeful, hungry look when I'm searching for a new place to live too. The first time we viewed someone's apartment in the city, the current tenants were all home, which is my nightmare. Their apartment was huge and gorgeous, it had a sunroom and two living rooms, a mini dining room, vintage appliances, and it was full of their cute eclectic vintage furniture (that was completely different from our haphazardly collected alleyway furniture). After ooh-ing and aah-ing for ten minutes, I noticed all the tenants posed casually in one of their living rooms conspicuously doing work on their laptops. Only none of them were actually typing or clicking around. I suddenly realized how awkward it was for all of them to bunch up in one corner of this huge, Perfect Apartment. They just sort of sat there, staring at their computers, poised to work, being as invisible as possible while I admired their furniture and planned to steal this Perfect Apartment from them.

Was this some sort of fucked up voyeurism? Seeing what other people have and being so convinced it's better than what you have that you must take it from them? I always feel an erotic stirring in the lower part of my gut when I'm in someone else's apartment. It's like crossing this threshold from the big anonymous normal world into someone's mind. Your home is inevitably a reflection of the irrepressible: your taste, your money, your habits. No matter how hard you try, you leave your mark, your residue on the place you live. Where the table is, where the desk is, the tidiness of your bed, the state of your kitchen sink, the errant book or sports paraphernalia or piece of junk you can't get rid of. The pile of discarded package wrappings, or the absence of them. Entering an apartment is an act of intimacy.

But here in the capitalist musical chairs game of apartment letting and re-letting, there's an undercurrent of pain and it's kind of cringe. Perhaps because we're all forced into this renting class, most of us are unable to buy property or move up economically, yet we're being priced out of apartments and neighborhoods we might have preferred to stay in. I go over and look for an apartment on a block that might be cheaper or offer more space and someone comes in to look at my apartment because they can easily afford the increased rent and will have the resources to fill it with bespoke furniture instead of with objects that someone else wanted to get rid of. It's compulsory movement, compulsory looking. It turns an act of intimacy into surveillance. Instead of a peepshow, it's more like you're a peeping pervert, some sort of freak who plans to steal someone else's home.

Don't get me wrong I'm no stranger to voyeurism. I mean, you kinda have to be okay with people gawking at you to enjoy getting Eiffel Towered in a gay bathhouse. And yes, I get a kick out of wearing a short skirt on a cold day and watching drivers slow down, rubbernecking to stare at me with confusion/disgust/intrigue. It's a not-so-secret goal of mine to look so hot that it causes a (non-fatal) car accident. Could you imagine?

Weird forced, real-estate flavored voyeurism. Like being in a fishbowl, under a magnifying glass, in an X-ray, surrounded by a surgical theater full of doctoral students, organs being priced for the black market. It's a different flavor of voyeurism—a piercing gaze. Having these strangers stomp around my apartment in their outside shoes, judging our piles of junk and slightly greasy oven, *while we're still living in it* is embarrassing. It's not the fun kind of people-watching at a busy cafe or in a park. It's like, this surveillance that turns us into contextless freaks, poor people that can't clean up after themselves. It's like the kind of surveillance that turns People into Others. The kind of incessant watching that turns trans people into perverts and monsters and makes me feel more like I'm being preyed upon rather than just looked at. Sized up. Maybe it's because in this situation, as the looked-at, I don't get anything out of it. When I strut down the street in a miniskirt and drivers turn their head as they zoom by, I feel like a star on the stage. Knowing that, like, ten people are staring at me and getting off while watching me get penetrated on all sides in a public shower feels more like a pleasure-multiplier, pleasure to the factor of thirteen. This voyeurism, this apartment viewing shit, feels like a reminder that we don't own this place we tried to make a home. A reminder that we're being pushed out against our will, that we're at the lowest rung of society's hierarchical ladder. We're bottom-feeders, and not even in a hot BDSM way.

* * *

Eventually, I followed a lead to Humboldt Park, to a hundred-year-old two-flat that was owned and managed by some family instead of a giant property manager. The place was slightly a mess—and the kitchen seemed like someone drew it from memory. A free-moving countertop was rearranged so that the oven could be closer to an outlet, which forced it to share an outlet with the fridge, the washing machine, and the dryer–the agent suggested that we use a power strip to plug all the appliances into one spot like the previous tenants allegedly did. Internet wisdom and common sense told me that doing so would result in an electrical fire. But I ignored that fact for a much more fun fact: this apartment had an in-unit washer and dryer! It was also just shitty enough, an apartment not yet so trendy and run by some guy and his nephew, so I knew that as the first person to see it, I was a shoe-in. Between the Prince, Audrey, and I—our credit scores averaged out to: bad. So, our previous apartment hunts resulted in rejection or required an excessively huge deposit to get in. This time, I realized how to get in: lie!

Once we were approved, and our lease signed, I got the key and let myself in to the apartment for the first time—our second place ever in Chicago. I was overwhelmed with pride and satisfaction: I found an apartment all by myself, through sheer willpower and cunning. I sat on the floor against the wall and ate a burger from across the street, soaking in my victory. We had a home.

A couple of months later, in the wake of my breakup with the Prince, I left the apartment to her and Audrey. Living with an ex, no matter how amicable the breakup was, quickly proved to be a bad idea, so I opted to couchsurf across the West Coast and hope that I'd land back in Chicago at some point, to an apartment I could call my home. Maybe after leaving Las Vegas and its shifting sands, I'd never feel at home again, at least not for a while. Maybe that'd be okay.

EVERY PLACE I'VE HAD SEX THAT WASN'T SOME-ONE'S BEDROOM

An abandoned house at the edge of the city. On the couch in the apartment he shared with his husband (sans husband). Harry Reid International Airport—Terminal 3 Arrivals parking garage. The Flamingo Hotel. The Wyndham Hotel. In his mom's house's garage. In the home office. In his children's playroom (sans children). In my Prius. In his mom's van. In an empty parking lot. In a full parking lot (security stopped us). In his flatbed truck. On the hardwood floor of his living room. On the hard tile of his laundry room. In my living room (sans roommates). In a hot tub. In a public shower. In the private room at a gay bathhouse. In the dark room of a gay bathhouse. Against the pool table in a tranny bar. In the bathroom of a Whole Foods. In the public bathroom at the outdoor mall (the one by Sephora). In the Western parking garage of the outdoor mall (the one by Sephora). In the parking lot in front of a fast food restaurant (too high to remember). At the hiking trail by the park (at night). By the dumpster in an alley behind an apartment building. Always in the shadows. Always in the periphery.

HOW TO FUCK YOURSELF INTO SOMETHING NEW

STEP 1: EGG

- Watch, watch, watch, watch. You don't know it yet, but you're already here.

STEP 2: LARVA

- Eat, eat, eat, eat the entire garden, go to the place where the birds live, the ones that might eat you, and eat there and pray that you don't get pecked for dinner tonight and squirm back to your flowerbed and keep eating.

STEP 3: PUPA / METAMORPHOSIS

- Destroy yourself. Unzip your body and pour out the contents, blend it all up, turn yourself into caterpillar soup. Use your ass like a pussy, fuck someone like you're wearing a strap, get fucked, feel the weight of someone thrusting against your dick, it is hard to tell who is fucking, who is being fucked.

STEP 4: BUTTERFLY

- You will emerge, wet and floppy, your body changed forever, your wings damp with birth, you will fly and fly and fly and you will realize you were a girl the whole time, and then you will lay the eggs, plant the seeds for the next garden and the next eggs, and you will hope they do not get pecked by birds, that they do not all die in a fire, and if they do, you will at least know that you became a butterfly.

NOT HAVING SEX IS A LOT LIKE HAVING SEX

I haven't had sex in a few months. I haven't masturbated in a week—longer actually. Don't get me wrong, I'm not swearing a vow of celibacy or anything. And actually, the last week has felt rather erotic. What first was a dry spell, a slow season of circumstance, has now become an experiment. An intentional fast. I've adapted something of an active posture of waiting. I'm sitting on my knees in anticipation.

Chicago is a deeply sexy city. As soon as I landed back here I felt a charge in the air. I exchanged a few stares with some burly men bursting out of their clothes, buff dudes stretching out their sleeves to the breaking point. Shirts cling tightly to fat bellies, and shorts around thick, muscular thighs. It's grey sweatpants season and everyone at the airport seems to be half aroused. Seemingly every woman at this airport is the most gorgeous woman I've ever seen, all of them idly lounging at their gates in cotton clothes that hug their hips, and I am simultaneously envious of their beauty and attempting to keep carnivorous thoughts at bay. I waited for my luggage to slide around on the conveyor belt, doing my best not to stare too hard at an androgynous punk, neon blue mohawk and square platform boots, whose bare arms are so shredded they look like they tear cops in half for a living.

I'm spending a week couch surfing with friends until I can move into my new apartment, but I can't help but open Grindr—just to check. Water the plants. You know. A few vulgar and over-eager messages trickle in, but they bore me. I like looking at genitals probably more than the next person, but I can just google a picture of a dick or an ass if I wanted. A long-haired man in the neighborhood sends something polite—*How are you?* —and subtly slides us into a sexty conversation about what I might do to distract him from his Zoom meeting.

Nice to know I still got it. I'd spent the last couple of months running around California in the aftermath of my breakup, healing and licking my wounds and trying to get my shit together. If, in the process of recovery, I'd somehow become an unattractive, sexless uggo in the unattractive, sexless suburbs of the Bay Area, I'd be very fucking upset.

* * *

One of the earliest lessons we got during my high school art class was about positive and negative space. Our high school art teacher, a four-foot-ten Jewish woman with long black hair down to her knees and impeccable comedic timing, projected slides of black-and-white charcoal drawings onto the wall. We were learning how to compose an image, what makes something interesting to look at—is this an image of two women about to kiss, or is it a vase? When it came time to draw, our teacher would gently reprimand anyone who drew the entire still life she had set up, all six Styrofoam shapes and drapery, the entire folding table. It wasn't interesting! Where's the vision?! I did my best to sketch something interesting—a Styrofoam orb rendered so closely it took up almost the entire page—but I was still a total noob. I knew what I decided to render was just as important as what I didn't, but it felt like a fucked up mind trick. If I actively think about the negative space, is it still something I didn't draw?

You can draw something, let's say a beetle, and bring it to life. The graphite produces legs, antenna, shell: bug. The carbon takes up space on the page. Graphite is enough to convince, but with paint it really comes to life. Phthalo blue, cadmium green, squeezed onto a clear palette and cut together with a knife, folded into a prismatic emulsion. This is the carapace, shining and hard. You can even put it into a little pink bikini—why not? You're in charge. Follow the instructions and you have produced an image of a beetle. The subject, the positive space.

But do you have a painting?

Maybe the beetle is this teeny thing, rendered true to life against a wide expanse of space. It sits, small, yes, but glimmering and full of verve in the corner. The other parts of the canvas, completely untouched, raw. The beetle is a beacon of life—it pulls you towards it. But it's the rest of the canvas, the empty space, that makes any of this interesting. What's all this space for? This tiny painted insect—how did it get here, exactly? The negative space intrigues. It invites you to fill the rest of it. Perhaps the beetle flew in from another painting, a world full of other shining beetles just like this. Maybe it's on an adventure. Perhaps the painting is simply unfinished; it's meant to be a forest teeming with creatures and little curling plants. Perhaps it's going to be a men's locker room, wet and salty, and the slutty little beetle is looking to cruise. Perhaps it will be a pantry stuffed with food, where the beetle becomes a thief.

I recently discovered the work of Bernard Tschumi's advertisements for architecture. He became interested in the works of architecture specifically experienced through advertisements—he realized so many people would only ever experience these grand designs through travel ads in magazines—images specifically constructed to stir feelings of desire.

Many of them strike discordant feelings in me, in the way that all good poetry and advertising does—it confuses me. One of these Advertisements for Architecture depicts a black-and-white print of a woman pushing a man out of a window. The facade of the building has intricate moulding, ledges on ledges of concrete maybe—but what's really important is this black silhouette of a man falling, seemingly from the open window. The caption reads:

To really appreciate architecture, you may even need to commit a murder.
Architecture is defined by the actions it witnesses as much as by the enclosure
of its walls. Murder in the Street differs from Murder in the Cathedral in
the same way as love in the street differs from the Street of Love. Radically.

There's another image that confuses me even more, there's less concrete to
grab onto, unlike the previous image which straight up commands me to
commit homicide. This one is in color, mostly inky black shadows broken up
by grey-ish blues, an amber orange something in the background. It's hard to
tell what the image actually is, maybe an interior of a building— somewhere
in the guts and liminal spaces. Perhaps a hallway for service workers in a large
building. Regardless, it's obvious that this is an image of empty space, some
vacuous backroom in a larger build. The caption on this one reads:

Sensuality has been known to overcome even the most rational of buildings.
Architecture is the ultimate erotic act. Carry it to excess and it will reveal
both the traces of reason and the sensual experience of space. Simultaneously.

I didn't understand what the ad was saying at first, but I felt compelled by it.
What does it mean to reveal the traces of reason and the sensual experience
of space? I think about the times that I've walked into a place and felt an
erotic tingle in my skin. The fresh, vacuum-sealed space of hotels make me
horny. A good hotel room is meant to make you feel comfortable—push the
aspects of a home into fantasy. So practical as to be impractical. Giant fluffy
white comforters and giant pillows on a giant bed, a giant window staring
directly at an expansive sunrise. Unlike the multi-functional bedrooms I've
lived in that have served as office, vanity, and dining room, sometimes all
at once, a hotel room is not for anything except sleeping and fucking. It's
the sort of purpose that you can feel in the very space itself—a feeling that
resonates down to your molecules.

For the second time in my life, I signed a lease in Chicago, sight unseen, from about 2,000 miles away. The previous tenant had moved into this apartment to heal from the end of her seven-year-long relationship, just like me, and I can't help but jump if things feel like fate. I saw the apartment for the first time the day before I moved in: the first place I've ever had all to myself. The previous tenant gave me a tour, then handed over the keys. The building is 100 years old, charming and slightly decrepit in ways that I love. It's also huge. The apartment spreads out from the doorway like a fan, three gigantic, rectangular rooms. It feels like a three-winged mansion. My friends, two incredibly fit jock-goths who I love dearly, move my small van's worth of worldly possessions up to the 3rd floor in an hour flat. The apartment is mostly empty space, my clothes and books barely filling a corner in each room.

One of my mentors told me recently about her pregnancy cravings. She told me that her hormones are not randomly generating weird and wild cravings like they do for women on TV. It was more that she had this heightened sensitivity to her own desires and the subsequent gratification of acquiring whatever it was she wanted to eat. The milkshake she craved on a whim became an epic quest, the acquisition of it downright euphoric.

I like the idea of tuning into my own erotic gauge, following a whim to its melodramatic core. I don't just want to suck dick, I want to slurp on a beautiful cock. I don't need to have sex, I need to get *railed into tomorrow!* If there is a way to not have sex in a hedonistic way, I think I'm doing it. Now that I'm really tuned in, everything in my life feels erotically charged. My finger strokes the edge of my PS4 as I unpack, and I realize how yonic it is. When I cover myself in lotion after a shower, I'm keenly aware of the hydrating sensation plumping up my skin, the sleek glide of my hands across my thighs. I write emails for work and get struck over the head with a vision of a past fuck, a naked torso, black curly hair against brown skin, a cycling unitard slipping down around his waist, the sudden pressure in my ass. While washing a mason jar at the sink, a memory resurfaces in which I'm stroking my friend's wet dick, slick with his cum.

The last week on my friends' couch discouraged me from freely masturbating —but going a few days without jerking off now feels like its own form of foreplay. The act of *not* doing something amplifies the act of *doing*. The negative space expands, bigger and more vacuous, and the potential for what could happen grows exponentially—so much could fill this space now that I have room to receive it. I wait on my new, old squishy leather couch, bequeathed to me by the previous bisexual who lived here, not masturbating, and wait for something carnal that I know will come.

Eventually.

FANTASIES THAT ARRIVED WHEN I LIVED ALONE FOR THE FIRST TIME

1.

I'm a giant woman and the entirety of you fits in one of my hands. I look down at you and you look up at me, and your eyes are dreamy, pleading. I gently place you in a tiny box lined with velvet and I shake you around for a bit. I place the box on the bed and wait for a while so you can catch your breath. When I open it up, the light from the room leaks into your little box, the light from the curtains that are parted just enough so that the room isn't pitch black, they fill the box you're in. You lay there, shaken up, breathing hard, and thrilled. I ask if you're okay and you nod.

2.

I am phone banking for a good cause and you are resistant to my canvassing, worried that I am a scammer or a bot. You google me and your tone shifts. I feel you leaning in through the phone. A month later you ask me for an update—it's a transparent excuse to talk to me. You're a little annoying and you say all the wrong things—but you lay it on thick, your interest. I ask if you have an ounce of cool in your bones, and you say you'll get on your hands and knees and beg for me to believe that you do. You're annoying, like a cat that doesn't know when to stop playing. I reach through the phone and kick you in the head. Later that day, I meet you for the first time and you pay for our dinner. You're better in real life. Your crooked nose leaks a drop of blood on the check as we leave.

3.

I ask you to come over and you come immediately. And then you do not cum again until I am satisfied.

4.

We are lying beside each other in my living room, under piles of blankets because I am collecting them for the winter. I wrap you up in the biggest duvet and roll it tight so that you feel your own hot breath against your face. Your arms are bound against your torso, but I've left your lower half free. I watch you struggle and kick your legs around. After I fuck your lower half, I unwrap you and your face is red and sweaty and you are smiling a big dumb smile and you inhale a sharp breath of cold living room air.

5.

I turn you into a bird so that you can perch on my windowsill while I cook. You talk to me aimlessly about all the trivia you know while I feed you bits of the vegetables I'm slicing. You don't mind that it's taking me two hours to cook this meal. When it's ready, we sit on the floor at a low table and marvel at all the dishes I cooked. I turn you back into a person and we share the meal together, gasping at all the flavors and textures. The meal stays hot, even though it takes us forever to eat it all.

HOW TO CAST A SPELL

1. Hold an intention in your mind
2. Perform a metaphorically resonant action with your body

e.g., Chant *I am a girl and this is my pussy* in your mind while you get someone to perform sodomy on your asshole.

e.g., Think to yourself, *I will survive* and then steal groceries from the store down the street and assuage your biting hunger.

e.g., In a world full of violence, commit yourself to building a world full of love. Throw a party with all your friends, eat together, and laugh.

When dream and reality align, the spell is complete.

WORSHIP THE BUGS

I love that fireflies only twinkle in July when it's hot and sweaty and they're all desperate to breed. I can relate.

From afar, a swarm of fireflies look like stars that have come down to Earth to party. A bunch of twinkling lights dancing around each other, down here for the summer instead of up in the night sky. Their signature glowing butts communicate a lot of things, apparently. Sometimes it's a warning signal to predators: *Hey, I taste bad, don't eat me*. Most of the time, it's used as a mating signal—a way to communicate desire and sexual compatibility between adults. I've always been fascinated by their light, and I love that we're not projecting romance onto them. Fireflies really use their lights as this nonverbal way to communicate their needs around sex.

But a firefly is just a bug—a set of spindly legs, a fat thorax pulsating with bioluminescent liquid. They're beetles actually, the same family as cockroaches, and they look like it.

I worry that I'm the same as a firefly. Look too closely and my shiny illusion dissipates. It's obvious I'm just a fat little bug stretching its antennae out in search of something, shooting out spotlights and asking to be fucked.

Now that I live where I can actually see fireflies, I'm more drawn to them than ever. I find myself hunting them down during summer, having prolonged daydreams about fireflies twinkling around the city. I ask Autumn what they know about fireflies, inquiring upon their mystical significance. Autumn knows everything.

Autumn tells me that the fireflies might be a feminine ancestor calling out and asking me to follow her. Maybe my femme ancestor has some knowledge to bestow, or wants to help me deepen my intuition. She tells me to ritualize my beauty routine in her honor. I'm a dummy in my twenties, in desperate need of knowledge and intuition, so I'm eager to commune with this predecessor.

Despite their indisputable insectoid qualities, I find fireflies very glamorous —they come out at twilight to sparkle and twirl around and disappear right when it gets too dark. I tell Autumn that my beauty routine has felt distinctly un-ritualistic lately, kind of sad. I've neglected this practice that I love, the act of changing myself into someone new, painting my outer shell with skin-nourishing goops and shiny pigments—the daily ritual of looking alive. Instead, my skin has withered into a dull grey, like my mood. I hole up in my hot bedroom at the far back of our long apartment, like a pupa in the brush. Now's as good a time as any for a glow-up.

My first summer in Chicago was spent late night partying, drinking, bar-hopping around town. I was eager for sexy hijinks, to shine my light and see what life in the city had to show me. I spent a couple of those nights at The Owl, the quirkiest and open-late-est bar in my neighborhood. It's the only one still open at two, three AM, so everyone still wanting to party makes the pilgrimage there from whatever other bar they were drinking at.

My memories of this bar play back like a montage from a late-90s sex drama, mostly because they're obscured by booze and drugs and sleepy eyes. Running across the street, short skirts, *unst unst unst unst,* someone screaming in delight, someone screaming in despair, lots of glitter, a jar of poppers, a tiny bottle of rum, a can of hard seltzer, go-go boots, dancing, dancing, dancing.

At The Owl, an absolutely absurd DJ played a set that flowed from psychedelic disco to Russian techno to what I think is a song from a Bollywood movie to Bad Bunny, finally disarranging the entire composition into a loose assortment of noises that might qualify as a song. In most of my memories, I'm alone on the dance floor jumping and spinning to the beat of the music. The quality of the music doesn't matter, just the volume and the BPM. I let the bassy waves from the subwoofer push me, push me, push me, push me until I can't hear anymore. The sound pushes me so hard my soul is shoved right out of my body, forcing it to follow behind me like an echo.

That first summer I beat my face for the gods every day, but at night I'd turn up the volume. Layer on more eyeshadow, more highlighter, so that even after dusk I'm radiating beauty. But it's hard not to feel like a clown amongst the sea of normie finance bros and cottagecore marketing girls who've started to infest the neighborhood. Even at The Owl, where the crowd feels the most mixy-mixy in this increasingly white neighborhood, I feel like the odd one out. In this light, fireflies don't look like stars, just bugs. Gnats. Roaches. Flies.

More than once in that Bacchanalian couple of months, I ambled to a table near the front of a bar, away from the strange music of the dance floor, and nursed my best friend's second, third, or fourth free drink of the night.

* * *

So many years ago I channeled the firefly in Vegas, a place where I'd never actually seen a firefly. Most of the time, I did my channeling at Hawk's, one of the city's gay bath houses—shaking my horny little thorax, looking to find some fun.

I was much younger when I crawled around that place, but I was something of a cruising prodigy. There's a trick: give into the liminal spookiness of it all. Turn the endless walking into a trance-like meditation, turn endlessly in the dreamy maze of rooms and glory holes and dark corners. Tune into the ambience: steam, chlorine, lo-fi beats. Some dudes are fucking nearby, everyone can hear it, but it's impossible to tell where.

At first, I'd repeatedly return to my locker to check my phone, wonder how much time had elapsed, see if anyone was messaging me. It took a while, but eventually I let myself loose, let go of minutes and hours. The fee to enter has already been paid and there are no refunds. Might as well stay until something fun happens.

Another trick to cruising: pay attention to the eyes. We love to talk about the poignant, silent gaze between lesbians in cinema, but fags have their own silent language of looking. I was always searching, peering into the eyes of old, white retirees, corporate regulars coming in after work, wayward blue collar gays of color, looking for something. A message. A returned glance. Flash of pupils. There's an entire language contained within the shapes of sclerae. But what I was really looking for was something that would surprise me. Someone not just down to fuck, but to play.

There's a dearth of conversation at a bathhouse, but it's still possible to signal, to flash the eyes, and find someone looking back. I evoked a mystique, a glamour, to see what playmates I could attract. At first, I wore my towel politely, snug around my waist like a guest at a hotel pool. Then I'd let it slide down to show off my soft body, my pubes. Eventually, maybe by lap six or seven, the towel sat around my shoulders, damp from steam. It's fun to walk around naked. I'd attracted a few eyes, strike up a conversation or two, but the spark wasn't always there.

During one visit, on my 10th lap around, a new guy entered the maze and it was immediately clear that he was the sexiest person in the bath house. I first caught sight of him as he talked to an attendant. His smile was so handsome it struck fear in my heart. His skin was rich and dark and seemed to glimmer in the dim light. His body was totally ripped, ready to shoot the cover of *Men's Health* or something; meanwhile, I didn't even have the nerve to shoot outside my league. I couldn't—can't—handle the rejection of being the third- or fourth-best option.

By my 17th or 18th lap I was still coming up empty-handed—this was sad, even for me. I sat in the hot water with everyone, closed my eyes, and silently absorbed their idle conversation while the water scalded my skin.

Hottest Man waltzed into the wet room and joined the party in the jacuzzi, sitting himself perpendicularly to me. I was eager to hear the bears and twinks flirt with him, hoping to sustain myself off of the erotic energy I'm sure would ensue. But after a short exchange, the bears and twinks excused themselves to go fuck somewhere else. There's no funny business allowed in the water—jizz being hard to clean out of a hot tub, I imagine.

Now it's just me and The Hottest Man On Earth. Out of boredom and with nothing to lose, I talked to him.

> *First time in here?*
> *Yes.*

He told me his life story, about moving to the city recently, about leaving the military. He was looking for the spots to have fun in town. He's surprised at how slow the bath house was that night, that no one was feeling him. I'm surprised, too, since he's the Hottest Man on Earth. He then said something to me that I carry with me to this day when I feel ugly, repeating it like a mantra, "I thought you were the hottest person in here. You look like the androgynous models in magazines." He asked me if I'm trans, or if I did drag or anything. At this point in my journey, I had not yet come into my girlhood, but I did tell him about being nonbinary, that I kind of don't care about being a man. He responded well. Chasers are sensitive to the blinking light of a tranny, even if that light is faint.

He reached out to touch my thigh, right by my knee. When I did the same, I was surprised by his extremely hard erection.

After we fucked, I shower. When I ran into him minutes later, he was fully clothed, on the way out. We hug awkwardly. I try to find him again every time I visit the bath house.

* * *

Years later, during my second summer in Chicago, everything feels pointedly less sexy. In place of parties and miniskirts and bottomless drinks, there is a breakup and a change in my medication. The political situation on Earth seems a bit worse for wear than last year. For a week, smoke from Canadian wildfires blankets the city in a throat-singeing haze. It was, mercifully, pushed out by a sudden and brutal storm system. But it didn't really feel like relief, just like flooding the floor of an apartment with water while the roof was on fire. Streets turned into rivers full of debris and crosswalks into unfriendly rapids. The rain came down like God was angry with us for fucking her shit up.

Firefly season should be starting, but they don't want to come out in the pouring rain. The conditions are too harsh for their delicate lights.

I have a new friend, and I think it's a date but I'm not sure. Our plans rest precariously in the hands of this tempestuous weather. We met IRL once, about a month ago, also in the middle of a deluge. That first hang (date?) we walked for miles, increasingly itchy and wet from sideways rain.

Luckily, the sky is kinder to us this time and there is no precipitation, no horrible weather to contend with. After a stroll around the wet park and a meal at a very mediocre Vietnamese restaurant, the two of us sit on the bed of his truck and smoke the rest of a joint. The first firefly of the season blinks into existence right before us.

I try to read my new friend's mind, looking into his eyes for some sort of message, but any psychic powers I might have are completely gone. Autumn says the fireflies are signaling me, but I don't understand what they're saying. I can't read his stare. Instead I feel stunned by the twinkle in his eye. I can't tell what the look on his face is: pity, lust, confusion, boredom? Maybe the hang's gone on too long. Maybe he regrets this new friendship. Maybe he wants to make a move. Nervously, I pivot the conversation to its end and head home.

The day's waning sunshine bursts through pink clouds, like a painting of heaven. A couple of puddles reflect pastel. The world has become all mirrors and light.

I walk home in this between-time, right after the rain at twilight, wondering where fireflies go when summer ends.

PICK YOUR IDOLS AND PRAY

You don't have to be a girl all on your own. Being a girl is an ongoing art project and all good artists have to copy someone else before they get good. These are my idols, to whom I pray:

My best friend Emma, my god of physical and emotional strength, my god of stability, my god of perfect eyeliner, I pray to you before battle and after. *Fran Fine,* my god of high-femme glamour, cinched with hair piled high, I pray to you before I ask my boss for a raise. *The Charlie's Angels (2000)* all at once, my holy trinity of girly hijinks, of disguises, of subterfuge, I pray to you before I infiltrate an evil millionaire's secret lair. *The Moon,* my goddess of change and moods, I look to you when I am empty and remember I will become full again, and I look to you when I am full and remember it will all come tumbling down soon enough. *Alaska Thunderfuck 5000 in episode 40 of Fashion Photo RuView,* my goddess of wearing eight inches of makeup with a plain T-shirt, I pray to you when I want to be beautiful and punk. *Viera, the fantasy race of bunny people from the video game Final Fantasy XII,* my pantheon of beast women, of elves in armored lingerie, I pray to invoke your mystique, your ethereal beauty, your Icelandic accents. *Cher in Moonstruck,* I pray to you when I need to believe in the wild irrationality of love. *My best friend Aja,* our conversations are a prayer, interfacing directly with God, or the universe, the thing that's bigger than us. *Fireflies, butterflies, cicadas, and bugs in general, honestly,* I pray to your vibrant, cacophonous yet short lives full of metamorphosis and sex and brutality. *To every girl who came before,* I pray to your audacity, your laughter, your beauty, your pain, your friends, your existence, when I need to keep going. *To every girl who has yet to arrive,* I pray to your audacity, your laughter, your pain, your friends, your existence, when I need to keep going.

STEAL YOUR GIRLHOOD BACK

Being a girl is fucking expensive. Even if you're one of those all natural, hairy-legged ladies, there are dozens of little purchases that you feel compelled to make. Personally, my transness manifests in the urge to play, to be a star. I love walking down the street and turning faces. It's pretty much impossible to tell the difference between someone who's staring at you because you look like a freak and someone who's staring at you because you look like a six-foot-tall goddess, baby. I like to pretend it's the latter. But, even if you're on the opposite end—seeking to be ignored, but ignored as a *woman*—you're going to need to invest in a couple of things.

If you're interested in transitioning, you're probably going to want to get some new clothes, and maybe a choker or two. There's the essential cost of nail polish, a manicure if you're fancy. There's the price of hair-removal tools, like razors or waxing or epilator or Nair or the hundreds you might spend on laser hair removal and electrolysis if you're *really* fancy. Maybe you'll invest in some bundles, to engage in wiggotry; a whip of horse hair in the wind goes a long way. Medical transition is pricey too, of course. There's getting to and from doctor visits and the cost of hormones. These little purchases add up to a small fortune, the price of being beautiful. The price of being treated with an ounce of respect as a woman, as a trans person.

It sucks that all the good stuff that attracts many of us to girlhood costs so much. But here's the tea—you can have a lot of this for cheap or free. Here's a lesson for you: every fantastic woman is at least a little bit criminal.

I grew up in Las Vegas. Naturally, all of my friends were hot girls who had a penchant for petty crime. Las Vegas really desensitizes you to shady methods of making money. I mean, the city has a dynastic mayorship, the

Goodmans. Mayor Oscar Goodman was the lawyer who represented the Mob. Like THE MOB, The Mob. He ran the city from 1999 to 2011, when his wife Carolyn Goodman promptly took over and is still, currently, the mayor of the city.

On my bus ride to school every morning, I looked out my window at a billboard on the freeway advertising directly to my high school:

HEY NEW GRADS AT LAS VEGAS ACADEMY, WANT TO MAKE SOME CASH? LITTLE DARLINGS IS HIRING.

When one of the upperclassmen became a dancer at Little Darlings in junior year, we gossiped about it. Not because it was scandalous or shameful; we gossiped enviously about how much cash she had—a fat stack of ones, fives, tens, and twenties, all earned from her shift the night before.

We grew up in the direct shadow of gigantic casinos, organized scams coated in glittering lights. We visited the dreamy, labyrinthine buildings designed to hypnotize people into spending as much money as possible, we watched people pour their money into ringing slot machines. If you stay long enough in Las Vegas you see that all of it is just an illusion. It becomes obvious very quickly that the only way to get what you want is to break the rules.

We started small, mostly with petty theft. My friends stole hundreds, if not thousands of dollars of makeup from Sephora. Why? Because we needed to look gorge, obviously. At this point in my life, I had not fully walked into my girlhood, but I was relatively gender fuck-y. While my friends stole supplies to do 25-step mugs[7] with primer, color corrector, foundation,

---

7   Mug as in mugshot.

powder, setting spray—all things talc-based and luxurious—I stole the kind of makeup that fags wear: duochrome highlighter, undereye concealer, glossy lip balm.

At some point, our little Bling Ring became notorious around the school and Emma, our Thief Lord, would receive bounties: requests written on little scraps of paper asking for Anastasia Beverly Hills, Urban Decay, Benefit. She'd swipe the goods and sell them for a profit. Our friend group became so good at stealing, that local Sephoras started hiring multiple security guards. We still succeeded, of course. Most security is just for show.

Makeup wasn't the only thing our five-finger discount applied to. Shoplifting had become so normal, we began to see the mall as a place to get cheap, if not completely free clothes; the thrift store as a giant closet to raid.

We learned that stealing from a department store was an easy way to get put in Mall Jail—they have cameras that work and a security team ready to arrest you. The dingy room where they stuff you in the guts of the building is not pleasant. Wal-Mart and Target do have a lot of security theater, depending on the neighborhood, and there's that rumor that their surveillance cameras are waiting for you to steal enough so that you're legally considered a felon before they nab you. I figure, as long as I steal a few toiletries here and there and make sure not to go over my lifetime budget of stolen goods, it'll be fine. If you're good enough at sliding things into your sleeves when no one's looking they won't come asking. Thrift stores that are also national chains get all their stock for free and are staffed by underpaid workers who don't give enough of a shit to keep an eye on things. It's a total racket. I feel it's your moral obligation to steal from them, in fact.

Here's how to steal from a thrift shop: come in wearing skimpy clothes, put on something you like off the rack, and walk right out. Alternatively, wear really baggy clothes and take your haul to the dressing room where you can hide all the clothes you want under your outfit. At one point I had a large varsity jacket from the defunct Nevada Electric company that I liked to call my Stealing Jacket. Not very creative, but descriptive. It had multiple secret pockets and voluminous sleeves with ribbed cotton cuffs that hugged my wrists. I would pull out my wallet from my secret pocket and use some sleight of hand to grab something off a shelf, using my wallet to disguise my mark from security cameras, then deftly hide both my wallet and stolen treasure back inside my jacket as if I hadn't stolen anything at all. I'd slip eyeliner and nail polish—or, when I was hungry and desperate food—up my palm and into my sleeve, where I stowed all my goodies until I left the store.

* * *

These years of teenage thievery prepared me for early adulthood. When I decided to publicly transition at twenty-one, I had a closet full of fag clothes. They had a femme tilt—lots of hoochie-daddy shorts and floral button ups—but they were still obviously the clothes of a gay man. I wanted to be a beautiful androgynous elf princess, so I needed to gather some threads.

When I started looking for jobs as my new self, stealing a new set of girl-clothes and makeup really came in handy. Early in my transition I balanced a remote writing gig making content for clickbaity YouTube videos, and a part-time gig slinging shawarma at Halal Guys. Basically, I put myself into a secret cocoon: away from the eyes of the public, serving food to strange tourists on The Strip, continuing to write internet drivel under my dead name.

That got old really quick, and the money wasn't good. I knew I needed to step up a ladder if I wanted to survive, *and* I knew I couldn't live life being perceived as a boy. I needed to be seen as femme, or even androgynous, with an ambiguous gender. I needed *glamour*. I started applying to office jobs because I knew I was good at computer work, and also because I could parade around offices in chic office lady-wear.

I didn't have a lot of experience, but I did have a look. All I needed was a good résumé. Once you're involved in petty crime, why stop at theft? Go for some light fraud. I lied on my résumé, extending every job I'd burnt out at, including the college where I dropped out, noting that I majored in Communications, or Art History, or English—whatever sounded the best for the job. When I got called for an interview, I'd show up in the grown-out boy haircut that I like to think looked like a chic little pixie. I'd wear this very cute brown corduroy minidress that women interviewers usually loved with a button up blouse layered over it—sexy secretary vibes, very competent office worker fish. If transitioning taught me anything, it's that a look tells a story. If you dazzle people enough with the way you tell that story, they'll believe you—or, at least like you enough to buy in.

It helped that the jobs I went for weren't super corporate spaces or anything. They were copy-writing jobs, advertising, or artsy non-profits, all in very small offices. Being a little kooky and creative-looking only added points in my favor. Sure, I'm pretty good in an interview, relatively good at coming across as competent, but I really don't think I would have gotten these jobs early in my transition if I wasn't wholeheartedly myself—visibly trans and queer, yes, but also dressed in very cool clothes. That I stole.

The reality of being a low-level grunt in the arts is you don't really make any money. In my office worker geish and face beat for the gods, I was hungry.

Making just enough for rent, just enough for my bills, and really not enough for anything else. This is where deft hands came through once again. The system we live in is not set up for trannies with no family support and no college degree and not a dime to their name to succeed. So, don't play into the system. If you want to be a trans girl, you might as well be happy, healthy, and alive. What's the point of all this makeup if I'm starving to death?

The key to stealing groceries is buying at least one thing. If you buy a bag of rice and an apple, you can pretend to scan a couple of eggplants, a carton of eggs, some cans of tuna. The receipt still prints itself out. If you slip a pack of steak into a reusable tote already full of your other crap, no one will really notice. Grocery stores with built-in food courts are great, too, because everyone just assumes you paid for that bag of chips and that can of coconut water. Just make sure you keep an eye out for security cameras, calculate their blind spots. Check out where security is lax and employees don't really give a shit. Be friendly, smile to the cashiers and the stock boys. They don't want you to get in trouble or starve, and they'll feel a lot more guilty about snitching on the friendly tranny who talked to them in Aisle 7.

You can tell rather quickly whether or not some place is going to be easy to steal from. If you're a girl with a little melanin in your skin, you've probably been tailed around a store, having someone stalk you to make sure you don't steal. Just because I'm *brown* doesn't mean I was gonna steal—I was going to steal because I don't respect the law and am broke! Totally racist for these store owners to think it was the first thing. Either way, their prejudices really get in the way of my stealing.

* * *

It's a lot of pressure to live a life of crime, to be the perfect woman. But don't feel guilty about it. You'll never have all of the right clothes, makeup, hair that will suddenly add up into an unclockable woman. On my fishiest days, where I fully believe I'm giving Cis Girl, I get clocked by two or three people. It's very humbling and a nice reminder that passing is a losing game. Cis women chase this perfection, too, and it sucks years off their lives. Embrace imperfection. Be a nasty, hairy, disheveled, woman. Be the kind of woman with perfect makeup and fucked up hair or no makeup and impeccable tresses of hair cascading down your back. Wear your mom's hand-me-down Prada bag with your sweaty polyester nightgown that you stole from Village Discount. Don't try to be a good girl.

The only reason that us queers of color are at the bottom of this totem pole is because white dudes set it up this way centuries ago. They pilfered, they stole, they lied, killed, raped, burned shit to the ground, and set it up so they'd be on top. I'm not saying you should emulate the White Man, but I do think that breaking a few of the White Man's laws can help you get up from rock bottom. How're you supposed to save money when you zero out your paycheck every month on food and rent? Imagine what you could do with the money you spend in one year on groceries.

Crime is not only something you'll have to get used to as a trans person, it's a part of our history. Transsexuals, transgender people—we all transgress against the norm. We have to break the law sometimes. I'm writing this while living in the heart of the Empire, smack dab in the middle of the United States. There's a concerted effort to scapegoat trans people, queers, drag queens, all of us weirdos and try to erase us from public life. The ACLU has declared an emergency on behalf of trans people because we're facing unprecedented, coordinated legislative attacks against our personhood, all under a Democrat president who seems to be asleep at the wheel. It's not hard to imagine a Republican president taking over and helping all these losers in their genocidal rage. Right now, I'm living in a perfectly legal transgender body. But next year I could be considered a criminal just for having a gender marker that's different from the one I was assigned at birth. Legislation could change the act of taking estradiol into a criminal act worthy of years in prison. But a life of crime has gotten me this far, it's gotten me my career, a loving community of found family and blood relatives. It's shown me unending happiness. All those years of petty theft, of illegal existence, prepared me for the ultimate act of criminality: girlhood. And since I've already committed myself to this life of crime, I'm ready to continue to break whatever laws the man will write to keep me chained up.

BE THE VIRGIN

In the beginner's mind there are many possibilities, but in the expert's there are few.

—Shunryu Suzuki,
Zen Mind, Beginner's Mind: Informal Talks on Zen Meditation and Practice [8]

I sat in the van, giddy and wide-eyed. Michelle and Sini dub Mya and me *tour virgins!* We were the only people in the car who had never been on a Sister Spit tour before. We were crisscrossing New England, from small town to small town, none of which I remember the names of. There was something in a city outside of Boston, a stint in Providence (I think), a show at a museum in New York (the performance was totally a disaster, followed by an exultant night at Russian Samovar with lots of dancing and smoked fish and potatoes and alcohol).

Before this, New England had mostly existed in rewatches of *Gilmore Girls,* in books about little gay boys in military prep school, in punk music. But now here I was, tearing it up through the original colonies with a bunch of queers in the middle of a wet and vibrant autumn.

When that sword fell on my shoulder and I was knighted *virgin,* a weight lifted from me, one that I did not realize I'd been carrying around. Michelle and Sini declared me—publicly, in front of everyone—a hot, young, uninitiated dummy. Here I was, on tour with Sister Spit veterans, people with published books and films, people with poetry zines and witch practices and semi-finished second, third, and fourth manuscripts that they were

---

8   I'd like to acknowledge that this is a corny ass quote and I have not read this book, but I saw it on Tumblr recently and it resonated with me.

carrying around. These people had stood in front of crowds and read their words many times over, something I'd only done once or twice at open mics at bars. What had I written beside a couple of whimsical emails? A funny Instagram caption?

During this tour, like most of my adult life actually, I felt like a total head-to-toe fraud. I've charmed my way into writing jobs, marketing jobs, non-profit jobs that I did not feel qualified for at all. I'd tricked everyone into thinking I was smart and writerly, despite never really putting any writing into the world, never studying the craft properly like everyone else.

But now none of that mattered, I didn't have to be a know-it-all, act coy when something went over my head. It was practically my job to be ignorant and open to anything. To ask dumb questions, to ask for reassurance, to let other people tell me what to do. To go along with the flow, to trust everyone to take care of me—I was a virgin, after all.

Once, when I was seven years old, I watched the glass table in the living room shatter, explode into razor-sharp snow. My mom and dad were talking, and it escalated into a fight as it often did. We'd moved into a small, haunted-feeling house in an obscure corner of Summerlin—some white supremacist's utopian project nestled into Las Vegas's edge. My parents were pulling a last-ditch effort at getting their lives together, even though they were so clearly not meant to *be* together. Our house, a relatively new building, was already haunted by a specter that gave me nightmares—the white supremacist's ghost, who surely did not want us to be living on *his* stolen land—as well as by my parents' cold and distant relationship, the surreal dysfunction of us all. At this point my parents had already decided to separate, to not be together. But despite their early marriage and two kids, they had trouble with commitment. They couldn't commit to the idea of separation, of splitting custody of us, so they un-separated and tried to live together again. So we all lived there in limbo, in that cold dark house in the corner of Summerlin.

I don't remember the fight that turned a sheet of glass into snow. I remember something shifting, the weight of conversation between my parents getting heavier, going to that dark place people go when they're overcome with disappointment or grief or rage. Then the table exploded. It was as if the energy of their conversation could not be contained between mere words anymore, the psychic weight of their exchange pushed and pushed and pushed for some release, like steam trapped in a vessel, like the momentum in a car crash, like a stray bullet. Their conversation shattered the table.

These conversations usually happened in a different room, behind-the-scenes, but their relationship always left a sort of residue in the air, palpable and heavy. It was not hard for my sibling and I to pick up on the harshness of the vibes. Dad's furrowed brow, Mom's downturned eyes, their feigned yet efforted interest in our childish questions about playing village, about being Pokémon trainers with us. Their marital conflict lingered like a ghost.

Only this time, with the shattered table, I was in the room when it happened. I didn't need to go ghost hunting. I knew in that moment, when our furniture became shrapnel, that I could not rely on these people to raise me. They were *messy.* They were *haunted.* These people threw tantrums. Other adults didn't throw tantrums like this—or lie, or spend hours crying into their palms.

What happened? I asked about the table, the table that turned to snow, and they answered with silence. The two of them morosely cleaned up the mess instead of saying sorry to me, or to each other. I decided then and there to get my shit together.

The thing is, I had no fucking idea what was going on, ever. Not when I was eight years old, not now. Still, I took pride in being the grounded one in my family and otherwise. In car drives or sleepless minutes during what was meant to be my nap time, I'd give my parents advice on dealing with each other and being empathetic, lessons I'd osmosed from children's TV shows and school. I tried to make up games for my sibling, tell them it'd be okay. I liked being the smartest kid in class so that I could give answers to the other kids, so that sometimes I could point out a mistake in the teacher's worksheet. Make things make sense for other people so that I could believe that things made sense for me.

On the internet, I often made friends with people who were older—one, two, four, years older—doing my best to posture at maturity. I'd flex my precociousness and access to a search engine and fudge my age. When someone would ask about my opinions on music or movies or art, I'd expertly feign half an opinion, parroting back to them their own. I'd pirate whatever music or movies or art they told me about, read the Wikipedia page and all the forums and all the reviews, look at SparkNotes, and Yahoo! Answers and form my own opinion—or, at least some amalgamation of the aggregate. I'd fall into relationship-y dynamics with people older than me, both offline and online. One internet boyfriend, six years older than me, was such a mess. I spent most of my free time in 9th grade texting him off the ledge, convincing him he should not kill himself, gently deconstructing all of his self-deprecation.

I liked knowing everything.

My illusion shattered when, after high school, all my prospects evaporated before my eyes. The art schools I applied to offered me *half* scholarships. Not enough to justify going out of state, and tuition and rent was so expensive there was no way loans would sustain me, either. State University was so mind-numbingly boring, and the required credits for every major I was possibly interested in seemed so rote, so beneath me—it filled me with dread to think about spending four years of my life pretending to learn about things I'd already known. I withdrew after one day.

Of course, I pretended like all of this was part of my own grand design, some wise choice to unplug from the system. Why waste my time and energy going into these fucked up schools run *by The Man* just to go into debt and emerge four years later the exact same way I felt now—confused, lost, and no career paths before me?

I proudly carried this know-it-all energy into my relationship with the Prince. So self-assured that I knew what was best for us at all times, our future. Knew what was best *for her*, and what she should be doing with *her* life, as well.

Whenever I *didn't* know something, I'd just turn to astrology or tarot. Finding answers in the randomness and patterns in the universe, sometimes talking out of my ass, desperately looking for answers I myself wanted to see. I needed to make sure I always had an answer, a fucking answer for every fucking question. Eventually, I was exhausted of knowing. My vision of the world, of my future, became narrower and narrower.

Being on tour with Sister Spit was the first break in this little façade, my fake expertise.

Sometime after the tour and after my break up with the Prince, I'd go full virginal. Let go of everything I'd ever known. My apartment, cat, relationship. This immolation felt pretty rational, I mean, I wanted to start over. I'd go to L.A., a work trip I'd already planned, then stay for a loooong time instead of coming home. I'd let my friends Ben and Jena take care of me, two beloved Tauruses who happened to live a ten minute walk away from each other. They housed me, fed me endless beautiful meals, kept me company. Between the two of them, I never had to make a decision about my schedule, didn't even need to make a decision about what food I was going to eat. It was like that for a couple of weeks.

After I was done leeching off my friends in L.A., Jena took me up to Yosemite with their college friends. One of these friends, Divya, was living in New York on a student visa, and had never been to California in her life. As we drove around the mountains of Yosemite, we all took turns giving her the lowdown—telling her about Californian geography, the spiritual effect that mountains have on people who live near them, the ins and outs of Californian culture. I saw how she took it all in, absorbing it all, and how the rest of us guided her along the hike. It was her turn to be the tour virgin!

* * *

At some point between being in a committed life-long relationship and being single as hell, I fucked a virgin. A private chef who lived down the block, a cute, chubby dude with fluffy hair and eager eyes, hit me up on one of the bouquet of dating apps I have on my phone at any time. He had definitely had sex of some kind before, but he had never had a real life, hard, flesh and blood dick penetrate him. He wanted me to have the honor of initiating him into the world of anal sex.

I was careful with him—gently fingering him, using his own spit as lube to massage open his asshole. Immediately before this he'd given me an energetic and very virginal-feeling blowjob (lots of teeth, not enough tongue).

I penetrated him, gently at first, then slowly getting a little more rough as I felt him open up for me. I don't have a lot of insight into the interior minds of straight boys who like trans girls, but I've seen enough porn to understand the general dynamics that seem popular—big tall trans girl makes small man her little toy, etc. I let my long hair cascade around his face, because I figure that guys who fuck trannies think it's hot to have a pretty girl's hair rub against their face while her dick is in them. If not hot, at the very least, it'd be novel.

Afterwards, his belly glistening with his own cum after a cute little prostate orgasm, we chatted a bit and laughed a bit. He promised to make me dinner with all his private chef powers, and I walked home. It wasn't even drizzling when I first walked over, but now it was pouring, and I realized that I forgot my umbrella at his house. I love my umbrella, short and candy red. A block away, I text him *Ooops, I forgot my umbrella!* Giving him the opportunity to tell me it's a good reason to meet up again or at the very least, run it down to me while I was still nearby. Instead, he read the message and promptly blocked me.

That fucking virgin stole my umbrella.

* * *

Despite being born under the sign of Virgo, I did not really understand the symbology for most of my life. Mostly, I was jealous of the other signs and their cool mascots—twins, sea goats, scorpions, lions. What was the Virgo? A girl? A *virgin?* Someone who hasn't had sex? It didn't make sense to me and mostly just resulted in teasing from classmates whenever astrology came up.

Eventually I came across the astrologer David Odyssey, who once described the Virgin archetype as defined primarily by the ownership and dedication of the body as a divine vessel, permanent outsiders whose powers come from their ability to define their own boundaries, private people who strive for perfection, who know when to show off and when to close off. He described the virgin as divorced from modern patriarchal connotations. While the modern idea of a virgin is an inscription of value on a woman—untouched, pure, meat for marriage. He discards all of that—*this* virgin is a devotee of her body, maybe she's voluntarily celibate, but the important part is she is someone who is choosing herself.

It makes sense then that in the tarot, the major arcana associated with the virgin is The Hermit. The Hermit retreats to his cave to write the perfect manuscript, to keep his mind pure of outside influences and find the absolute truth in the world. In another version it could also be The Nun, a woman who retreats to a cloister to be free of what she previously knew. No pressure to perform, no pressure to be a Woman. Instead, she is a virgin dedicated to herself, to spirituality, to God. In abandoning her worldly possessions, in the devotion of prayer, the monotony of chores, she empties herself and becomes a vessel for something new, holy, and weird.

* * *

There are many times when I have felt like a complete and total dummy. A baby. A beginner. The same way 5th graders act like know-it-alls to 4th graders, seniors act like big shots around freshmen, I think we go through these cycles of feeling like we know it all and feeling like we don't know shit about fuck. Right now, I'm knee deep in the complete dummy phase. I feel so liberated by this, by the weightlessness of being curious, being uninitiated by the world. Single, in my late twenties, exposed to the grand horrors of this world, no cat or partner or family to make sense of my life, I feel like a wild animal crawling around, raw instinct and intuition. My expert façade is completely shattered, turned to snow, disintegrated, and my heart is left pulsating and exposed for anyone to do anything with. But, I think I'm okay with this. I do not want to be one of those people whose heart is hardened and closed, whose feelings are hiding in a box inside of a drawer, deep in their spirit. I like this new life, constantly confused and devastated and elated and surprised. I have accepted my role as the virgin, the Virgo. I can feel the world rushing in, alive and wet. For once, I am finally ready to welcome it in, ready to engulf me, ready to spend whatever years I have left on this Earth dripping and throbbing with life.

OPTIMISM WILL BREAK YOUR HEART

The sky is appropriately grey because I am consumed with ennui. I like when the weather matches my melodrama. At Dunkin' I am greeted by a sole employee who appears to be tending to this donut shop by herself. To be fair, ennui is already ebbing at the edges of my brain for reasons that I will perhaps be ready to talk about later. But something about the grey sky and the empty Dunkin' drives me all the way to the place in my heart where the best pity parties get thrown. I smile when I order, but I do feel like I could just start crying in the middle of asking for an apple fritter.

A loud man comes in and it's hard to tell if he's yelling at me or the employee or at someone in his Bluetooth headset. I think both the employee and I are worried that the delicate serenity of this empty fast food joint is going to be ruined by an evil customer. Because I am a polite girl quietly crying as I eat my tater tots, I do not believe my mere existence is ruining this lady's lonely shift despite the fact that I feel guilty for being a customer and existing in most retail spaces. Loud Man harasses the Dunkin' Lady for a bit and generally yells into the open air of our Zen garden. I worry that this will be a permanent vibe shift and my silent crying will be more like a panicked crying.

Loud Man does leave, though. And in ten minutes we both relax again, I fully settle in with my iced coffee and *A Little Devil in America*. Hanif Abdurraqib tells me about Afrofuturism and his mother singing along with Patti Labelle's girl group from early in her career, Labelle. In this chapter Hanif is talking about a performance where Labelle is singing from some undisclosed location in space with beautiful black hair and space suits, looking casual and cool as they belt away. Hanif is talking about the times he saw Black people in space on TV, and I'm imagining a beautiful future where the humans that visit the galaxy are melanated. To be incredibly simple, the whole thing with

Afrofuturism is that it is incredibly healing and incredibly fun to imagine a future in which white supremacists did not win.

Back on Earth, here in this Dunkin', the employee—I'm really sorry I didn't read her name tag—sings to a song I don't know. In the lobby, they're playing *NSYNC from what I assume is a corporate-approved Pandora radio station, but back there her phone plays a different song in a different language that maybe reminds her of her family. But who am I to really say? Maybe she just likes Bollywood songs. I listen to Filipino disco and it reminds me of my family and home and makes me feel safe, but I've never been to the Philippines at any time, let alone during a time when disco was popular. My parents listened to Aegis (who, by the way, rule) if they listened to songs in Tagalog but mostly they liked Journey and The Eagles and Michael Jackson and Cher.

My life is full of people who love me and sometimes I cannot see them and I do not call them and they do not call me and I try to send a text and sometimes we talk for ten minutes and maybe that's enough. And I'm holding back tears in this Dunkin' because I want to become friends with the woman who served me an apple fritter and I want to tell her sorry for intruding on her alone time at work when she could sing to her music and clean and look at her phone and I wish I could feel loved all the time but sometimes you can practice gratitude for what you have and still feel like you've been abandoned and that perhaps you don't have everything you need.

I'm a graduate of Tumblr university where so many selfless bloggers posted their therapists' advice and all the poetry and psychology and philosophy they were reading and so I know that it'll behoove me to sit with feelings of sadness. I try to remember what I learned with my Tumblr undergraduate degree and resist the urge to wash all my bummer thoughts away with a beer or weed or candy or dating apps and I just wonder why we have to be lonely when we all have each other and the only thing separating me and the employee at this Dunkin' is a two-foot-long plastic counter?

I think that's why the dating apps got to me, why the rejection and the ghosting stung so much. That's how the game is, dating and slutting around. Not everyone wants a piece. Maybe it's because I'm delusional, but I believe that every one of us could be connected, good friends, family, lovers, if the circumstances were right. If we tried. That every time something doesn't work out it's a failure of this timeline—two of us humans just estranged mammals incapable of communicating. And I guess I'm saying I could be convinced to take a bullet for the Dunkin' employee but what would hurt more is that, in this scenario where I'm taking a bullet for her, some other human shot the gun and how can it be true that we are all the same species when some of us are so malicious and murderous and mean? And maybe if someone held a gun to the employee at this Dunkin' and I had a knife I guess I would stab the shooter in the chest and somehow his death would be better than hers. And I don't understand it at all.

Rejection is a big feeling for me to deal with. It's not like anyone is really good at dealing with rejection (unless you are, in which case please let me have some of your magical power) but for me, being rejected brings up complicated feelings. It is what many may call a "trigger." At least that's what I learned during my aforementioned time learning stuff on the internet.

Growing up as a fag enshrined my life in rejection. I tried make a home in the big empty space void of being left behind. Teenage fags are left out in so many ways—we're the first to be excluded from our beloved girl-dominated friend groups. I've always loved hags and always will, but hags can occasionally leave a fag behind, intentionally or not. All-girl sleepovers might immediately bar a fourteen-year-old gay boy from entry, as it has for me. Back when I was a straight up fag, and not the kind of fag that takes estrogen pills, I had been left behind once or thrice while my friends took a group visit to the girls restroom. It's hard to look casual when everyone around you gets up at once to go pee. And of course, there's the ever-present rejection of being a fag son to a semi-violent dad who would have really loved a non-fag son.

Teenagers are horny little bottles of pent up emotions, and sometimes fags interact with bicurious boys who like to tap at the glass but never really want to see the specimen up close. Cute first kisses, gentle teen romances—these sort of things aren't really within the domain of a young fag. What I'm saying is, faggots get left out and maybe that's why we all get so cunty. Or maybe I'm saying *I* got left out a couple of times and now it's trauma I carry around like a heavy purse.

After a while, a fag stronger than this one might have gotten accustomed to this sort of regular exclusion, a subtle ever-present rejection, used it as a power or something. I only became more sensitive. Another *no*, another *not good enough*, another way that the shape of my body and my personality were just wrong for the occasion.

When a fag becomes a tranny, a lot of things start to make sense. We start to fit into places we always wish we did—in the magical community of women and dykes and other trans girls. But in a lot of ways, the frequency and volume of rejection goes up exponentially. Especially these days, anti-trans sentiment is pervasive and constant and *loud*. It's in the streets, it's in the news, it's on your phone. Sometimes, you don't feel like a woman, you feel like an advanced level faggot. And sometimes it's like, *Fuck yeah I'm a faggot!* And other times I'd like to become invisible, irrelevant, and I'd like people on TV to stop discussing the validity of my life.

And I don't want or need anyone to feel bad for a lowly tranny such as myself, but I just want to maybe figure out why I feel so afraid to sit in this Dunkin'. It's not that I can't be alone, but that I'm heartbroken no one's chosen me. In this particular minute of this hour of this day, I'm no one's priority. I am alone, crying with tater tots and coffee and a donut.

There are so many kinds of heartbreak, so many volumes and shapes and flavors and colors. There's the hard stop: a breakup, a *"No."* Then there's a million other ways to feel pushed out: there's *"not now."* There's the halfhearted *"yes."* We've all been someone's *"I guess, why not."* It doesn't make you feel lucky for being chosen, it makes you feel like garbage that someone's deigned to pick up.

I'd like to stop being a romantic and fantasizing about meet-cutes and tender love and a meal paid for and chivalry and thoughtfulness and enthusiasm. I'd like to stop looking so that I can stop feeling that familiar feeling, the shattering of a dream.

Before I transitioned there was a dullness—not happiness, *definitely* not happiness—but an ever-present sorrow that pushed at me through a thick layer of cotton. Horrible, but bearable. Because I was asleep to some truth about how I was and how the world was, everything didn't hurt. As much. And maybe taking estradiol gave me the visions of the swirling vortex of the void at the center of the earth that made me so prone to episodes of ennui, or maybe it's because enacting my own free will upon myself and the world helped me to open my eyes too. Transitioning moved me from that soft distant pain into a place that allowed me to access greater joys and more happiness than ever before. It ripped that protective layer between me and everything else. Along with that bright and shiny fucking joy, came a deep and bottomless pain and sadness.

And I guess I feel lonely in this Dunkin', but when I'm having a picnic in the park in a big flowy dress or when I'm watching a gag and a stunt at a drag show or I'm watching my friends play a video game over the internet and sending them encouraging texts from my laptop, I can feel like a part of something big and beautiful and fun. And maybe the saddest part is not everyone gets those glimpses of community and being together and joy. I promise I'm grateful, I'm grateful.

But, alas, not only am I trans. I am unfortunately an optimist. It's kind of in my nature to compulsively believe in a better version. A better, more complete version of myself. A better version of my life. A better version of other humans who not only treat trans people with tolerance or indifference but, perhaps, love. Big and loud. Even now, I can't help but dream of it because it feels so close. And I just want to be friends with this woman at Dunkin'.

MOTHERHOOD IS NOT A CHOICE

I tend to attract people who want me to be their mommy. There's something about being a six-foot tall woman with hips that could birth an army and a dick that could sire one that makes people think I can take care of them in all the ways they want, like I'm some kind of somatic therapist that will heal both their Oedipal and Electra issues. I used to have a sort of faint disgust when anyone approached me with that desperate look, a whining tone in their text message. The puppy dog eyes of someone who needs a tender hand over their heart and a firm fuck in the ass; the dating app messages full of men and women begging me to step on them. The thing is, I guess, I do kind of like being a mom.

There's this thing they made me sign at the free clinic where I first got my hormones, an informed consent form. This is what everyone has decided is the most ethical way to start treating your gender like a chemistry set, barring handing out meds and needles to anyone who asks. It basically goes like this for everyone: your physician or doctor or nurse practitioner or whatever will ask you invasive questions about your gender, to which you should respond in easily quantifiable responses. *Does continuing to live life as the gender you were assigned at birth sound disconcerting to you?* Oh Yeah, Totally. Suicidal Vibes Over Here if I Don't Get Estrogen. *How long have you been out socially?* For, Like Ever. I Just Need This One Final Step To Become a Girl.

It works best if you feed The Man an easy trans narrative—the person with the stethoscope does not want to hear about your unquantifiable gender identity, how you don't necessarily want to live life as a cis man or cis woman, how you're kind of more on a monster/goddess/fairy princess vibe and you just want to grow some boobs and get a prettier face. The metanarrative around us is that we are women trapped in men's bodies and medicine is the key to our jail cell. And listen, maybe that makes sense for you, but it doesn't really for me. *I'm a woman trapped in a man's body?* That doesn't even make sense. I was a loose parcel of molecules that slowly formed itself into the shape of a baby, and then slowly ate through the world until it became an adult person. This man and woman shit is all after the fact, language and words and culture that we have woven together. Maybe I'm more of an actress assigned to a role to I don't really *vibe* with. Does that make me eligible for estrogen? Can I get a role-reassignment? Where do I get recast? But, depending on who you tell your princess fairy dreams to, depending on what year it is, who your doctor is, what color your skin is, what state you happen to be living in, these fantasies could land you in some sort of conversion therapy program, an in-patient torture room where they electrocute the princess fairy dreams out of you. It's probably safest to retell that easy truism about being a man trapped in a woman's body.

I do not say any of this to my nice physician's assistant, her perky blue eyes and her thick blond hair. She is a medical professional who has chosen to practice at a free clinic in a bad neighborhood to give medical advice and prescriptions to families that do not speak English, and to trannies like me that want estrogen. I tell her I have Gender Dysphoria, and I would like some hormones, please. Dr. Blondie hands me a thick packet of paper that tells me everything that could happen to me if I get on hormones and leaves me alone to look it over. She is probably attending to the quadruple-booked patients in adjacent rooms, but I take the alone time anyway.

This informed consent packet is a list of things that some doctors *think* is true and *might* happen to you. Gender diverse people have been around forever, and the modern medical model of transsexuals has been here for like, a century, but they still don't know shit about our bodies, or how hormones affect the brain, let alone the soul.

Changes that will be PERMANENT; they will not go away, even if you decide to stop hormone therapy:

• Breast growth and development. Breast size varies in all women; breasts can also look smaller if you have a broader chest.

• The testicles will get smaller and softer.

• The testicles will produce less sperm, and you will become infertile (unable to get someone pregnant); how long this takes to happen and become permanent varies greatly from person to person.

Changes that are NOT PERMANENT and will likely reverse if hormone therapy is stopped:

• Loss of muscle mass and decreased strength, particularly in the upper body

• Weight gain. If you gain weight, this fat will tend to go to the buttocks, hips and thighs, rather than the abdomen and mid-section, making the body look more feminine.

• Skin will become softer and acne may decrease.

• Facial and body hair will get softer and lighter and grow more slowly; usually, this effect is not sufficient, and most women will choose to have other treatments (electrolysis or laser therapy) to remove unwanted hair

• Male pattern baldness of the scalp may slow down or stop, but hair will generally not regrow.

• Reduced sex drive

• Decreased strength of erections or inability to get an erection. The ejaculate will become thinner and watery and there will be less of it.

- Changes in mood or thinking may occur; you may find that you have increased emotional reactions to things. Some persons find that their mental health improves after starting hormone therapy. The effects of hormones on the brain are not fully understood.

Hormone therapy will not change the bone structure of the face or body; your Adam's apple will not shrink; the pitch of your voice will not automatically change. If necessary, other treatments are available to help with these things.

xxxxxxxxxxxxxxxxxxxxxxxxxxxxxxxxxxxxxxxxxxxxxxxxxxxxxxxxxxxxxxxxxx

Sure, some things are true: my chubby boy boobs blossomed into tender little girl boobs that sing at a hard pinch or toothy bite. My mood and perception of the world changed, the sensation of my body and my mind transformed into a new shape and a lot of the dysphoric noise in the background of my head felt relieved. I could see a little more clearly.

While I do know some trans girls who lost their ability to get hard— nympho girls whose sexual propensities leveled out after transition—some of this shit will simply not apply to your own journey. For instance, my own sexual libido has waxed and waned over the last couple of years rather than simply receded. Although I'm not sure how much of that was related to my hormones and how much of it was related to being dirt poor, living in run down slum buildings, trying to survive a pandemic, or the boom and bust of my long term relationship. Now that I'm older and I've gotten a little bit of a stronger grip on my frontal lobe and a relatively stable foundation upon which to build my life, my sexual libido is at an all-time high. I'm about seven years into my chemical transition. My dick will get erect if the wind blows the wrong way, pulsating at the slightest touch of someone hot or at the mere mention of someone's erotic adventures. My testicles are still:

huge, big, and dangly. I can ejaculate hard enough to fill a shot glass on the other side of the room. I also wonder if sexual libido really recedes or if, in the process of navigating your new body, blowing up everything you once knew with tiny blue pills of estrogen, that sort of ego death and surrender changes your approach to sex. Plenty of girls I know are still horny as ever, just a little more protective of their space and their bodies, giving less of themselves to the erratic and dangerous hunger of utter strangers, seeking more profound sexual adventures, the kind of connections that resonate mind, body, and soul. The kind of sex that lays waste to your mind, shakes up all the molecules in your body. The kind of amazing sex that lingers for days, weeks, and years.

* * *

Before I transitioned, I never really wanted to be a parent. Parenthood was not something I concerned myself with or aspired towards. When I was twenty-four, Mollie had gotten together with her girlfriend, Cassi, and our two-bedroom cave was too small for two fully-fledged couples. When our lease was up, my partner and I moved from that slummy apartment into another slummy apartment, this time with my sister, just three blocks away.

In this apartment, my partner and I did our best to parent my sibling. I'd felt guilty about leaving them behind at my dad's house for a year and a half. When I moved out, my dad got worse. He went unchecked, pushing my sibling's boundaries further and further until they basically didn't exist anymore. They'd become a nuisance to my dad, an obstacle to the life he wanted to live. I hated myself for leaving them there, and after I moved out, they spent a lot of time sleeping on my couch and having dinners at my place with Mollie and the Prince.

When we moved in together, I did my best to take care of her, to try and undo the damage our father did. To give her the freedom to become a person, to become herself. It was hard, considering the Prince and I were practically still children, reeling from our own parental neglect, trying to raise each other. But I felt a duty to protect my sibling, this person I loved; to tend to them, water them. That's beautiful about queers—we raise each other. We listen and care and feed and house and witness each other in our full, embarrassing glory. My own childhood was buoyed by my internet friends, the queers I roleplayed family with from halfway across the country. We came to each other for advice, for wisdom, to be seen and held when we could not see or hold each other. I know so intimately what it's like to be cared for and to care for others; how that love can keep you from falling over the edge.

* * *

After Dr. Blondie approved my scrip and I first started estrogen, I experienced a prolonged euphoria. I remember glowing, seeing everything around me in a sparkly technicolor. I'm not sure if this was a side effect of the hormones or if it was a feeling of catharsis. It was like I'd been craving this dish, some exotic hamburger or stew that I'd never been able to try before, and now that I'd finally gotten to taste it, the sensation exceeded all boundaries of my imagination.

After a month or so of that emotional high, I started to feel these pangs of darkness. I remember this heavy feeling rising up like a tide, slow and ebbing, up from the bottom of my gut, down again, up to my heart, down again, up to my throat, down again, until one day I found myself surrounded by this swirling darkness.

I sat in my dark apartment, that first, cave-like dwelling behind a Best Buy I shared with Mollie and the Prince, staring out the window. Could *every* girl see this mass of energy, the life force of everything on the planet slowly draining into the core of the earth? I'd suddenly become so extremely aware of the cyclicity of life, how we live and die and live again. I received visions of humans across space and history, people connecting and then killing each other, then laughing together and sharing a meal, then starting wars. I sat there, slumped against our hard IKEA couch, paralyzed, watching us do this over and over and over again.

It was fucking scary.

As a so-called "boy," pre-transition, it's not like I was disconnected from feeling. I was a total crybaby, sensitive to the horrors and tragedies of the people around me. But this was a different level, a total, head-to-toe, embodied devastation. It's as if I *was* everything around me—I was my friends and my ancestors, I was the cacti outside, I was the pigeons in the parking lot. I was them, and I felt every single one of their births and their deaths, and every inch of struggle in between. I was paralyzed, and full of the void.

The Prince came out and found me quietly crying as I stared at the window.

"What's wrong?"

I started really sobbing, trying to choke out any words. "I'm hungry," I said. "I really want to eat some chicken tenders." I know that this all seems like an obvious hormone swing, some shallow delusion that could be filled with calories, but to me this vision was real, like I could *see* it so clearly. I reached for chicken tenders, the salt and the nostalgia and the protein, to latch myself back into my body and away from the swirling pool of oblivion.

If everyone with estrogen pumping through their bodies couldn't see this, this overwhelming empathy with others, this psychedelic one-ness with the world, I was sure that other trans women could at least. There was this feeling of connection to everyone who has ever lived and died and struggled on this planet—but also, I felt like I could see every trans girl before me standing on this precipice, the world between worlds. After that vision, a clarity and understanding washed over me. Every radical transfemme that I'd read about, watched documentaries about, seen in YouTube videos, their fire, their grief, their wild optimism and care—it was survival. I'd read about these third gender, third sex, intersex, nonbinary roles across so many Indigenous cultures. Identities that explode the whole binaristic gender role assignment thing; people who aren't necessarily *deviant*, just living outside of,or in some blend of,the feminine and the masculine. In the Philippines, baklâs are a whole archetype of flamboyance and glamour, something Westerners see as a blend of gay male identity, faggotry, queendom, and transfemininity, and these people—my people—are often vessels of unadulterated joy, of beauty, of sex, and of care.

When house mothers in the ball scene built families around their children, when Sylvia Rivera stood in front of a mob in New York and yelled at them about caring for trans girls, it was coming from this place of vision. I was so sure that they'd all seen the swirling void too. They'd seen the cycle, they'd felt the deaths and births of all their friends. They felt themselves in their friends, in their ancestors, in the cacti and the pigeons. These transfemmes had fiddled with their body like a chemistry set, watched their mind and body change before them, and realized that we were all just amalgamations of microbes and chemicals, shaped by the people who had touched us. Their radical activism was community care, yes, but it was also a desperate struggle for self-salvation. If we are all one, then saving someone else from suffering, from needless death, is saving yourself from one too.

* * *

Now I'm starting to get a rush, a laugh, whatever out of the whole mommy-kink thing. Whether it's some fucked chemical thing in my body kickstarting some reverse-Oedipal complex in my brain, or because it's just my role in life as a giant woman to swaddle people, I kind of like it. I like being the big spoon, making this big, fleshy shelter for someone to hide inside of. I like cooking for someone after sex; I like aftercare. I want to step on your fragile body, I want to hurt you in a way that feels unsafe, because you trust me not to hurt you in a way that you do not want. I want you to suck on my tits like you're a hungry little baby desperate for milk. I chose to be a mother when I started taking estrogen, but now I choose to be a mommy because it's hot.

The people in my life who have given birth tell me it's like interfacing with the void. Like they've opened up this portal to the abyss inside their bodies. Here's an exercise: try to remember what life was like before you were born. Whatever that reality was like, it's going on in the womb. Whatever comes after we die, I think, is like that too. Oblivion. The people carrying babies in themselves, they're interfacing with that—being pregnant is dangerous. You're building life inside of you, and it could kill you. Complications from pregnancy, medical malfeasance, or lack of care, the dice rolls wrong and results in a miscarriage. Death, pain, injury, it's all swirling around pregnant people at the same time as life, joy, and euphoria. At least, that's what I see. I've never had kids, will never grow a baby inside of me, but if that estrogen-fueled swirl of void energy is anything close to pregnancy, then it seems like interfacing with oblivion, reckoning with death, is essential to girlhood. Transitioning is a motherhood too. It's the creation of a new self, the construction of something completely new from loose pieces of fabric, history, molecules.

Estrogen gave me access to another kind of death—la petite mort. Pretty decent trade-off if you ask me. If I have to become witness to the blackhole of life and death and the center of the planet, at least I get the gift of full body orgasms. I'm not super sure if there's a correlation to that scary sight of oblivion and the chemical access to the orgasms that rattle your ribcage, squeeze screams from your body like toothpaste, force your brain to relinquish control, turn you into an animal incapable of higher thought. It's nice—if our entire outlook is going to be wracked with existential dread, we can also be ravaged with pleasure. A gyrating vibrator to the groin, a fleshy orifice sliding up and down your wet junk, a digit pushing up against your G-spot, shoving you oh so close to the edge, oh so close to that void. Acknowledging the death of everything in the universe, the plants, the pigeons, my friends, my family, myself; well, it only makes me feel more alive.

* * *

The first time I put that tiny blue estradiol beneath my tongue and let its chalk dissolve into my gums, I became a mother. It's unlikely that I will procreate biologically—again, not because I can't, I'm so virile I could singularly fill all the vaults of a sperm bank—just because it doesn't feel right. Making a baby requires so much work, luck, healthcare, and emotional baggage that I maybe don't feel prepared for. I've got a lot of ancestral baggage, already. I have that whole obligation to mother-every-gay-person-in-existence-thing going on. I want to leave behind a memory for trans girls, advice and hope for trans girls to live. I want to be a good trancestor. I want to be a steward for young queers and for this earth, to take care of her like she's taken care of me.

For us, motherhood is not a choice, it is an obligation. Once you see that swirling void of energy, once you see that nothing separates humans from animals, you understand nothing—not the cruelty of capitalism, not the decimation of war, not the violence of gender binaries—is predetermined. We can make it stop. A milligram of estrogen can change your entire body. A little bit of clarity could change the world. That milligram of estrogen, that skirt over your dick, the eyeliner on your face, also marks you as different. These choices say: *Fuck you* to the status quo. It says, *I will choose my own happiness over my safety.* It leaves you vulnerable, it does not let you hide behind a false cisgender mask of being a normie. It leaves you open to being destroyed by The Man. All you can do is pick up the gauntlet, become a mother, steward, parent, guardian and try to protect this earth from all that cruelty, and hope that it does not destroy you before you can destroy it.

* * *

BORN AGAIN, AND AGAIN, AND AGAIN

Before I was a girl, I was a dream.

Las Vegas is a land between the dreaming world and the waking one. The city thrums with life 24/7, doused in eternal light. In the summer, a collective sleeplessness bewitches everyone in the city—locals and tourists alike. The heat radiates into the night and becomes inescapable in the darkness, no more shade to find relief from the sun's fire. The sensorial difference between night and day is even blurrier. We are propelled into neon-soaked all-night diners, pleather karaoke boxes, dimly lit bars, nightclubs shaking with sound. In the summer we are neither nocturnal nor diurnal; instead, we are ever-awake wanderers in artificial mazes of games and dancing and drinking and wandering.

The world projects onto Las Vegas an idea of opulence and luxury, so it becomes true, the city is a place for indulging and gambling, sailing up through skyscrapers, and an endless meal at a buffet. But the city struggles against itself. There's a version of Las Vegas that wants to be a shining glamorous star, and there's another version that crawls towards entropy, towards natural equilibrium, towards a slow life. Cacti eagerly gulp up rainwater that comes in floods and then meditate, unmoving for weeks, months, so as to live. Houses and hotels and malls and parking lots keep expanding out from Las Vegas's core, The Strip. The valley aches for implosion, for the city to break under its own weight so that it can become a desert again, not a false oasis. The earth beneath glass giants reaches for its next breath.

This is the place where I was born.

That's where I was born—in that glittering concrete mirage—but I made my first entrance into this world a bit off-stage. There's a small town outside of San Francisco, one that is somehow colder, wetter, and foggier. Filipinos, Mexicans, Chinese—immigrants who had just come to America along with families who have planted their roots for several generations—make their homes there. I haven't been back in a few years, but when I was younger I remember all of us taking shelter from the weather in mid-century modern shoebox houses. These houses were safe against the mist, always lit up with the warmth of potlucks—folding tables lined with kaldereta, pinakbet, sinigang, lumpia, lechon—the air full with ballads of Celine Dion and Aegis. Breakfast was always fluffy pan de sal dipped into mugs of hot chocolate or instant coffee mixed with condensed milk. Food was plentiful, even if some days it was cold Vienna Sausages and rice or instant ramen boiled on the stove. It always felt like enough. I don't think I saw a white person for the first ten years of my life—but that was probably for the best. I was born on these hills, into a family of families in The Bay, safe from the piercing gaze of white Americentrism.

This is what the sky looked like when I came into being: the sun aligned with the constellation of Virgo, the maiden hermit obsessed with purity and devotion, obsessed with the feeling of obsession, how it charges the body with an electric current, a divine possession. The moon sat beneath Cancer, the sign of the sensitive mirror and the crab who builds a home wherever they go. Capricorn rose to the east, the sign of hard work and hardship and dancing with the devil. My Venus, the hot planet of love and beauty, aligned with the glamorous sign of Leo, inscribing my heart with a desire to find a world that will look at me and worship. These stars sway slowly in constellatory unison, watching over our own solar dance through space. The planets and asteroids and moons in our galactic neighborhood spin around the sun in predictable patterns, in a movement that has lasted eons, and yet they still find new contours in their never-ending dance. I was born at this exact moment in the song: Virgo sun, Cancer moon, Capricorn rising.

When I was nine years old, my family immigrated from the safety and stasis of our hill in the Bay Area to take a bet on a house in Las Vegas, a place fertile with opportunity for anyone optimistic or deluded enough to try and make something there.

In this new city, space was plentiful. Our cul-de-sac straddled the edge between suburbs and wild desert. I was equal parts shy and crybaby, a little too awkward to understand classmates who did not grow up in the same Filipino enclave by the sea. I spent most of my time at home with my sister and with our toys. Together, we played make-believe and constructed worlds full of joy and adventure with tiny plastic Pokémon. For a couple of years, this is how we coped with the loneliness of the desert. But, we'd soon get a family computer—which, I quickly discovered, functioned as a portal directly into dreamland.

With a computer, my make-believe world grew bigger and more vivid. I logged onto massive multiplayer online roleplaying games where one's entire self was projected onto tiny pixelated avatars. In the muddy, medieval world of *RuneScape*, I could be a pig-tailed witch that lobbed magical icicles at goblins while hiding behind boyfriendsin-shining-armor. In *MapleStory*, I could be a cherubic anime pretty boy with twinkling eyes and curly brown tresses cascading upon my head, taking care of all my friends with sparkly green healing spells. The internet as we know it now perhaps feels like a giant freeway with cars flying by at sickening speeds, crashing over each other and into each other and spilling out of control. But back then, it felt like a *place*. I remember it not as a mêlée of social media, but as a bunch of forums that felt like interconnected rooms, each dedicated to one obsession or another.

In one room, back down at the end of this internet hallway, I found a role-playing group of people acting out a niche iteration of Pokémon characters in a private boarding school and asked to join. These strangers and I tried on different masks. We'd roleplay as characters for a couple of weeks, drop them for another set of characters, return to old masks, abandon those. We played together and got to know each other, unbound by space or by our bodies. Years passed and we remained friends, talking constantly through our laptops and phones. Despite the distance between us, it felt like we were always nearby. As we got older, many of us transitioned, embracing new names and bodies in the real world. But in our virtual friend group, this didn't matter much—our years of playing had primed us to accept and love the shifting of identities, the trying of new masks. It was in these chatrooms, floating through cyberspace with my friends, where I was born.

* * *

By the time I entered high school I had the gumption to channel my Leo Venus, to be a little more of a social daredevil. But despite my wonder, I found school to be rather oppressive. A lot of boring, rote, busy-work that most people could learn by having a passing interest in the world around them, by visiting a public library, or reading Wikipedia. Depression drained me of my will to try and often shoved me into the hole of my bedroom, playing video games. But even with the company of my online friends and my sister, I wasn't shining the way I wanted to. There was a hunger deep in me that I could not sate, a powerful draw to be a part of the world, and for the world to know me.

It didn't help that my parents had divorced, and my dad had nearly full custody.

My dad had a penchant for hurting others. He liked to actively sabotage my life—and the lives of everyone around him—with sudden, angry tantrums and financial abuse. He loved us, so he said, and then he'd say, *If you love me, you'll help me out*, and he would say that when I least expected it so there was never a discernible pattern. He would say, *We're really fucked, unless you have a couple hundred dollars* on the second to last day of the vacation I saved so much money to go on, making sure I had no money to feed myself until I came back home, and no savings to come home to. He would say, *I can't do this on my own* and drain my bank account, take my entire paycheck, use my social security number to get fake jobs and cash *those* checks, too, and take out loans and credit cards in my name, making sure to squeeze and squeeze until there was nothing left. All with my permission—given freely, out of love. He would tell my sister and I (and I'm sure my mom, and I'm sure his next wife, and the wife after) that an unloaded dishwasher, a floor that had not been mopped in twenty-four hours, an errant dust bunny, was proof of our failure, was proof that our love was not as vast as his love for us. He would tell us of our failure loudly, until his eyes were red and his forehead bulged, until a glass was broken against the floor or until everyone in the house had sufficiently groveled. His love built a world for my sister and me that felt tumultuous and riddled with disaster. In the morning he might be charismatic and doting, showering us with affection and food and hugs. By the afternoon, he'd berate us for only completing ten household chores and forgetting to finish the eleventh one he'd just made up. He'd come home angry with us for sitting on the couch when we should be in our room, for being in our room when we should be cooking dinner, for cooking dinner when he had surprised us with takeout after work. His fist would find something to destroy—a window, a wall, a car, my cheek.

Everything in my father's life has to orbit around him, and if it didn't, it was some aberration of nature, an affront to the laws of physics. He'd slowly set up everyone to rely on him—friends, coworkers, children, girlfriends, wives. He was the provider, he was the house, he was the food. He'd ask for small monetary contributions, just a show of appreciation for how much weight he carried. The asks would get bigger and bigger. The money he asked to help make ends meet would then become regular bills that he wanted us to pay—and would mysteriously get larger. His car would get newer, shinier. The living room would be remodeled with a new set of leather couches from the furniture store, bought on credit. He drained everyone around him of their love, their money, and their time. In this world, my dad was the weather, and you prayed for a day of peace and not a storm.

The world outside of my dad's seemed bleak too. When I was fourteen years old, I'd won a lottery to get into an arts magnet high school, saving myself from one of the worst public school systems in the country. I feel grateful that, by complete chance, I was given the space to learn how to paint, write, and see the universe with an artist's eye. But I had a hard time reconciling my hopes and dreams for a career in the arts with reality. America was dealing with horrific acts of police brutality, with the fallout of rampant climate change, with a rising fascist oligarchic power in the United States of America. Hasn't it always? Maybe the answer is to stop searching for the magical medicine that will fix America, and instead, find a way to end it.

I felt like a powerless teenager with little ability to do anything good for the planet on a large scale. I'd eat vegetarian—vegan, if I could; I'd recycle and learn about social justice theory, to spread the good word of bell hooks and Karl Marx. As I did this, the news stories kept coming: the police kept beating people up and the rainforest kept catching fire. I spent a lot of time disengaging; pouring myself into my painting studies, into my internet life, the realm of dreams and ideas rather than this material world whose only abundance seemed to be in its limitations and scarcity.

But I wanted to spend all of my time in dreamland. When I was seventeen-years-old I began studying the ultimate form of escapism: lucid dreaming. It's a phenomenon in which you become conscious within a dream and, to some degree, gain an ability to control it. I'd done it a couple times purely by accident. In the middle of a dream I'd realize I was hanging out with one of my long-distance internet friends IRL, and the impossibility of the situation snapped me out of my dream's spell. Suddenly, I could jump on a bus with my friend and go for a ride, pull out a sword and start slicing through walls. The power was intoxicating. I'd thought lucid dreaming was something that just happened occasionally, not something you could control. But one day on Tumblr I came across someone's blog about their adventures in lucid dreaming and realized it was something one might be able to do on purpose.

I read old witchy blogs from Web 1.0, trawled through subreddits, even picked up a gigantic, thousand-page collection of Freud's theory of dreams, on clearance at Barnes & Noble, to figure out a formula for consistent lucid dreaming. Every night I'd go to bed early, trying new methods to trigger lucidity. Many nights ended in frustration, in failure—or I'd come close, only to become too lucid and wake up completely. But eventually, I concocted a ritual that would nearly always work.

First, I'd lay on my back and stare at the ceiling. Then I'd create something I called an "anchor." This is a distinct object that draws me into a dream while simultaneously helping me wake up from its illusion. My favorite anchor was a red convertible—something I'd never driven but could easily imagine. I'd visualize cruising down a highway in that red convertible, top down, hair flowing in the breeze. Laying in the dark on my back, I'd silently chant:

red car, red car, red car, red car...

This rhythmic meditation would eventually get me to a sleeping state and kickstart my dream. Because red cars and driving along highways were on my mind, that's where I'd be in my dream. Once in the dream, I'd have to maintain a Zen state—-aware that I was dreaming, but suspending my belief just short of logic waking me up. There's an invisible barrier at the edge of consciousness that separates interior from exterior. One must approach this barrier with caution or risk popping right through. Lucid dreaming feels strange, like peering off the edge of a sheer cliff. It requires the acknowledgement of the barrier between dream and real life while simultaneously demanding that you ignore it. To stop myself from falling over the edge I'd focus on the front of my head where the third eye would be and imagine a small, still pool. This would reinforce that border and keep me in my waking dream.

Once I'd gotten a grip on this Zen state, I could do whatever I wanted. I could fly, I could shoot lightning from my fingertips, I could talk to ghosts. I'd materialize in the foyer of a luxurious, abandoned mansion and explore its depths, scavenging for secrets and treasures. Sometimes, I visited a version of my high school that was underwater, where everything was the same but better—less hot, less alienating.

* * *

When I graduated I moved out from the constant hurricane at my dad's house. In my first apartment, shared with the Prince and my best friend Mollie, we could build the lives we wanted. We didn't have much, but what we did have we spent on food, clothes, decorations, toys, and each other. We played games together, had fun, cooked. Life was not a never-ending maelstrom of anger with brief respites—it was full of joy, all the time.

It was in this apartment where I first became Vera Blossom, where I started my journey into girlhood.

There was, I think, no better place for me to construct this new self than Las Vegas. The city is a malleable landscape, a sort of stage where any dreams one projects can become reality. It builds new neighborhoods and malls and behemoth resort hotels because it wants to, caring very little about the amount of water, infrastructure, native people, or wildlife that existed before. It's a city that pretends Lake Mead is a never-ending spring of life, not a slowly depleting reservoir that diverts water from Rocky Mountain snowmelt. It sees the flat expanse of the Mojave Desert as a blank canvas to build whatever image it wants. Even remnants of its past that don't jive with the new Vegas aren't safe—historic buildings like the Stardust and the Aladdin are gone now. The city blows up buildings that no longer match whatever image they want to project this decade —literally rigs them up with dynamite and implodes them, turning them into dust in minutes. Within days, they erect something new. It was here, in a city of destruction and construction, where I was born.

The city taught me to destroy parts of myself I no longer wanted people to see, and point twinkling lights at the parts I wanted them to notice. I chose to erect monuments of femininity and humor and killer eyeliner, and suddenly those would be the parts people remember. We don't see Las Vegas for its bones—the blue collar workers running back and forth behind the scenes to keep the show running, its imported food and streets clogged with cars. At first glance, the desert does not look full of life, there are no burrowing night owls or coyotes, no endless acres of brush and cacti thriving for decades, just expanse. Instead we see the fantasy: the luxury skyscrapers and architectural marvels, giant spotlights, and dancing babes glistening with sweat. We play up the city's Mob history but pretend like it's not still run by criminals and profiteers. We see $25.99 seafood buffets 400 miles from the ocean and Michelin-starred plates of steak. We see alcohol and parties and prostitutes. We look directly into its 10,000 lux light. But it's all an illusion. Not the glamour or luxury—that's all true. The trick is in only showing only one half of the story. Everything is still there, in between buildings, at the edges of suburban expanse, sleeping dormant under concrete shells.

Now is a time of upheaval. Capitalism and labor rights are both in the forefront of our mind as mega corporations stretch themselves thin, extending their insidious tentacles into a growing number of aspects of public life. I see not only the growing capitalist overreach, but the entropy coming for it. I see that the weight of capitalism's dream is becoming too heavy to hold itself aloft. We feel it in the air: the weather is breaking down under the pressure, the fabric of social life ripped apart by profit, our collective psyche anguishing. Perhaps we're becoming aware that we're inside of someone else's dream—that it is a nightmare. The dream has long been dead and now we're living within its carcass, putrefaction swelling it with rot. But what comes after bloat is the breaking down into smaller pieces, the something-dead being turned into seeds for something alive. The body implodes.

When strangers look at me walking down the street, they don't have to see a fag in hag's clothing. They might see a tall, glamorous woman. They might see a trans girl. But they see what I show them: short skirts, perfect makeup, long hair. They don't have to see the hour I spent shaving my body, or the mood swing my meds caused me, they don't have to see the version of myself with a beard and a blond undercut, they don't have to see the crybaby. But those versions of myself are still there, lying under the new buildings. The dust of my previous incarnations provide material for the new one.

* * *

I feel like I'm being born again here, as I write this book. Building a version of myself that makes sense in the wake of loss, a loss of something unplaceable. I think I'm at the edge of my girlhood, right before the end. There are some points in our life that we might think of as the end of a childhood: an 18th birthday, a high school graduation, the acquisition of a driver's license, or the first day at your first job. But I think perhaps childhoods end suddenly, and when you least expect it. That first loss of innocence, when the full weight of your life—the world, the universe—presses down on your heart. I remember a few of those moments: when a fight between my mom and dad ended in the shattering of a glass table. When I maneuvered family politic, starting a catalog of secrets and lies in my head to keep track of. There was something taken from me when I watched Black Lives Matter protests one morning during my 11th grade history class, the rage and hurt of generations of violence burning in my body. That same year we began thinking about college seriously, and I knew I wouldn't be leaving my hometown anytime soon. I remember the first time I had penetrative sex, a decision driven by pure lust and hormonal teenage hunger; disappointment and darkness permeated my body with every thrust against my ass.

Those were losses I felt so clearly, in my body. Now, after a decade of reclaiming some of the dreaminess and playfulness I perhaps should have had more access to as an actual child, I can feel the ending of this phase. The end of my girlhood. I'm in the ending of a seven year relationship, a partnership that I jumped into at twenty. I used to make fun of other people who got married young—not me! Instead, I U-Hauled with a person I was in love with, moving them across the country to live with me, committing my life to our livelihood, sharing resources, an apartment, building a life together. Totally different than marriage.

I grew up in a city of facsimile and collage. The Strip was Venice, Paris, it was an Arthurian castle, impossible glass skyscraper, tiger gardens and pirates, all on the same five miles of road. I lived my life half on the internet, half in real life. Partly dreaming, partly awake. I spent hours reading Wikipedia like a book, playing video games, yelling with schoolyard friends. I'm pretty sure all of this has leaked into the architecture of my brain so that my own thoughts are collage, a mishmash of time of and style, a crosshatch of this make-believe land and the real world.

I'm trying to write an autobiography and I can't find the tone: somewhere between ironic jokes I read online and the most sincere, heartbreaking poetry that I love, love, love to let destroy me. Trying to make sense of this life I've been living, and maybe, in doing so, I'm building a blueprint for survival for other people like me. The kind who are passionate and lost, who are looking not just to survive but to *live,* the kind of person who has had so much taken from them.

* * *

I had so much fun lucid dreaming my teenage years away, so much fun that I feel guilty about it. So many hours spent sleeping and running away. But it felt *so good.* Now, I think, I try to emulate what that felt like, I put on my little outfits and walk around the world projecting this storyline onto them, re-writing the narrative into something more fun around me. Maybe I became a writer so that I could stitch together the universe I found in those dreams and the material world I find when I'm awake.

Reading about a place is like conjuring a mirage. To go to that place in real life is to feel its edges, the molecules lined up in space, to reach out and touch it. But you can go somewhere without seeing it. To make a place real is to feel its existence. To lay one image—the dream, over another, the material—and see in kaleidoscopic vision the present and the past and the futures.

Growing up, Las Vegas asked me to see the residue of all who have passed through—the entertainers, hustlers, criminals, day laborers, capitalists, tourists, burrowing owls, coyotes, cacti, sagebrush. It asked me to see the beings who had given their blood as an offering to keep up the spell. It asked me to learn the myth: the cowboys of the desert, the high-risk gamblers who bet everything and won, the sex workers who used their wit and their body to survive, the service workers who poured their sweat in to keep their family afloat, the hare who used to race on the land before asphalt was poured in, the ichthyosaur that used to swim through the valley when it was underwater years and years ago.

The city asks me to buy into all of that, the drama of its past. But then, I have to ask: what does the future look like? It's hard for me see anything but one possible conclusion for a city with so much hubris: destruction. The only thing that makes sense for a city like Vegas in a world that's burning up like ours is one where it is in ruins. One where it is smaller, where the desert has taken back some of its space.

* * *

I've died many times before. There was the death of myself as a five-year-old, sensitive and prone to crying, killed when I was told many times to stop crying. There's the death of myself as a thirteen-year-old, shy and preferring the interior playland of my mind. The death of the teenage nympho faggot, who sought validation and connection in sex with strangers in strange places. The death of myself as a twenty-one-year-old, the new girl flailing through femininity, attempting to find a world in which I could experience gender euphoria and financial stability. Now, with twenty-seven years of a life in this body—ten years of abandoning the gender binary, seven years into a social and medical transition—in a new city hundreds of miles from where I grew up, I feel myself changing again. The shedding of a girl and the metamorphosis into a trans adult. Someone whose heart aches for things past and works towards a better future. I carry the grief of plants, animals, people boiling alive in the global heat of capitalism. I carry the love of trancestors before me whose heartbreak and hard work I can feel so deeply now. I hold a light: the knowledge that things can change, the body can heal. I see beyond the lines that separate the dream world from the material world, the body from the mind, humanity and wilderness. The border between our planet and outer space, the border between molecular life and organisms—it's all malleable. It's all fractal. We see how the planets in our solar system dance around each other, repeating billion-year cycles like clockwork, yet changing and changing and changing. They say Venus once had a climate closer to Earth's before it went through its own global warming. Saturn's been spinning for billions of years, but its rings of asteroids are only a hundred-million-years old, new additions to its old routine. Our very own planet has gone through stages of molten heat, frigid cold, and lush life. I believe in the earth's ability to heal. I believe in humans' ability to change, to come together, and to assist the earth, our mother, our family, ourselves, in healing. I believe in an internet that connects us, challenges us, creates a vibrant dreamworld that we can all be together in. I believe in an earth that reverses global warming, that recuperates dying species. I believe in building something new from the ashes of our old world. I believe in something better.

My goal here is to conjure a mirage of a queer utopia for our time, or maybe to open a portal into the world I see, the one I've found in my dreamland, a vision of our planet that is full of love for all its beings and for its earth. I want to call upon the girls who did not survive, who were murdered by someone else's fear of beauty, and to remember them. I want to love them now so that their spirits can breathe life again. I want to call upon the girls in the future and tell them to keep believing, that all it takes is for us to keep believing. I want to remember all of the joy that trans people, people of color, have sent into this world. All the parties that have carved out a space for happiness and togetherness in a world full of nonchalance. I want to build an infrastructure in our imagination for a queer utopia. Once we believe in the mirage, this glamorous loving future, once all of us are having the same lucid dream, maybe then, the gap between our imagination and our reality will cease to exist.

GRATITUDE

Thank you to the pantheon.

Thank you, Michelle, fairy godmother, for building a world I could play in.

Thank you, Ann, Tanaïs, my literary shepherds, for guiding me into my own heart.

Thank you, to all my teachers, for seeing my light—even when I didn't—and tending to it.

Thank you, Emma, my sister, my rock, for teaching me how to steal.

Thank you, Aja, my soulmate in this lifetime, the lifetimes before, and the lifetimes hereafter.

Thank you, Mom, giver of my flesh and blood, my model for faith and everlasting change.

Thank you, my Sibling, for showing me how to be brave, always. I love you forever.

Thank you to my Fated Family, brought together by chance and bound together by love.

Thank you, to The Groupchat: Summer & Lille, without you I would be so much lonelier.

Thank you, to the Prince, for being there with me, through it all.

Thank you, Ben, for your healing, your friendship, and opening your home to me.

Thank you, to the girls who came before, all the girls still here, and all the girls yet to come.

Thank you, to every crush I've ever had.

Thank you, to the fireflies.

ABOUT THE AUTHOR

Vera Blossom is a proud Filipina American and transfemme monster. Her work explores desire, pleasure, gender, and death. She writes the steamy, confessional newsletter How to Fuck Like a Girl, and cofounded Snack Report, a food blog focused on rituals, feelings, and friendship. In 2021, she helped produce Black Mountain Radio, an artist-driven audio project published in collaboration with Black Mountain Institute and the *Believer* magazine. In 2022, she was associate producer on season 2 of *The Anti-Trans Hate Machine*, which focused on the disinformation ecosystem constructed by the Christian Nationalist movement. In 2023, she was selected as an Ann Friedman Weekly Fellow and a PEN America Emerging Voice.